pg 4

37
41
42
44

D1306136

Foreign Exchange
Risk

Foreign Exchange Risk

Andreas R. Prindl

Morgan Guaranty Trust Company
of New York

A Wiley — Interscience Publication

JOHN WILEY & SONS

London · New York · Sydney · Toronto

Copyright © 1976, by John Wiley & Sons, Ltd.

All rights reserved.

No part of this book may be reproduced by any means, nor
transmitted, nor translated into a machine language without the written permission of the publisher.

Library of Congress Cataloging in Publication Data:

Prindl, Andreas R.
   Foreign exchange risk.

   'A Wiley—Interscience publication'
   Bibliography: p.
   Includes index
   1. Foreign exchange 2. Risk 3. Hedging
(Finance) 4. Corporations — Finance 1. Title.
HG3851.P76   332.6   75—37684

ISBN 0 471 01653 5

10 9 8 7 6 5 4 3

To the memory of my father
Dr. Frank J. Prindl

Acknowledgements

Any book covering a field so varied, both in the problems it presents and the reactions of firms to those problems, represents the comments and improvements of many individuals. I am indebted to Morgan Guaranty Trust Company of New York for allowing me time to work on the manuscript, for its general encouragement of this effort and to a number of colleagues within the bank who read all or part of the drafts, in particular John M. Stadter, Jr., John P. Garber and Frank B. Arisman. John F. Ruffle, Comptroller, and Thornton D. Strecker, Deputy Comptroller, of the bank helped in technical accounting and tax areas. On the other hand, the book represents my own views and does not necessarily reflect the position of Morgan Guaranty Trust Company.

Corporate readers of draft chapters included a number of financial executives who themselves deal with foreign exchange risk; among them were Robert K. Ankrom of Chrysler, R. Geoffrey Bardsley of Xerox, Richard K. Goeltz of Seagrams, John J. Manion, Jr. of CBS, Kenneth S. Richards of Cavenham, Maurice D. Taylor of Alcan Aluminium and Nicholas Wheeler of Cadbury Schweppes. All of them provided valuable input from the practitioner's viewpoint. Alan Shapiro of the Wharton School's Multinational Enterprise Unit made some material corrections and improved my understanding of academic work in the field. John E. Broyles and John S. N. Drew of the London Business School helped similarly. Remaining errors, of course, are entirely my own.

I also owe my family a considerable debt for putting up with increasing irascibility, my parents-in-law, Dr. and Mrs. Peter Koerber, for loaning me their house in Mondsee to write in, and Marjorie Jackson for typing and retyping beyond the call of duty.

London
December, 1975
ANDREAS R. PRINDL

Contents

CHAPTER 1

The Role of Foreign Exchange in the Firm

The massive growth of international trade in the 1970s, and of multinational corporations serving as the main conduit of that trade, has not been an organic development. The multinational companies, which are now at the heart of a heated debate as to their motives and effect on local economics, have not grown into large homogeneous units, as the casual observer might believe. Rather, their growth has led to *fragmentation* of these internationally dispersed companies, which tends to increase directly as a function of their size.

This fragmentation comes from a number of structural and environmental factors, and accentuates the problem of managing the financial function of the firm. Impediments such as distance, unreliable communications and different time zones are well-known. Structural elements of exchange control, other regulatory barriers and different tax systems have become increasingly important for the management of international companies, particularly in the financial sphere. As the global expansion of firms carries them into new locations, this structural complexity is enlarged: each country of operations will circumscribe the actions of local affiliates, depending on its own monetary and financial policies.

The evolution of the firm itself can add to the fragmentary structure. The company not only expands into different markets, but develops different technologies and employs personnel of widely different nationalities and temperaments. This multiplicity of economic, political and social forces has widespread implications for basic corporate objectives and strategies.

The increasingly difficult field of foreign exchange risk management adds to these structural and environmental problems. The assets and liabilities of international companies, by definition, are held, and their income stream achieved, in a variety of currencies. While the latter have always been subject to relative changes, bringing potential losses or gains for the company, the situation has been exacerbated by the advent of floating rates in the early 1970s. Exchange risk management, not always a well-developed function in the firm, has become critical both for the protection and utilization of assets and in the overall planning function.

The term 'exchange risk' has several meanings. 'Accounting risk' relates to the necessity to value disparate assets, liabilities and income items in terms of a single currency. The risk element is that the publicly stated value of the company's assets, equity and income may be adversely affected by the movement of currencies in which it has dealings. Translation losses in terms of the base currency can reduce its reported profits and diminish its nominal net worth. The corporation's image may be thought to be endangered and its stock market appeal diminished.[1] Some finance executives may feel that their ability to raise loans or equity is thereafter put into question. Certainly there is a risk that a firm with large translation losses may appear less well managed than others in the same economic position which have borrowed only their own currency or covered all translation risk.

For example, in 1974 a U.S. office equipment firm reported foreign exchange losses over the year of $15.8 million, primarily from the appreciation of its sizable foreign borrowings. A U.S. food products firm of similar international size and penetration reported a 1974 exchange gain of $935,000. The questions which such a disparity between firms raises are, first, is there an important distinction between the results, and implicitly the management, of these companies, and secondly, could such effects be avoided?

From another viewpoint, not all of the accounting losses reported by a firm will have actual operating significance. The company may over time consolidate a number of asset or liability items at different closing rates, items which will never be converted or which will be renewed and maintained constantly. As ongoing elements in a subsidiary's financial structure, there is no tax effect to restating them in terms of a parent balance sheet; they can be seen as permanent features of the group abroad, as long as affiliates are not liquidated. Losses on their translation in the U.S., U.K. and other countries where consolidated accounts are published, cannot be offset against pre-tax income.

Some companies will regard the risk of adverse accounting changes as ephemeral, depending on their own stockholder structure and perception of risk. Translation losses might be seen as more of an embarrassment, or, depending upon how they arise, as an unavoidable cost of doing business abroad. The firm may be regarded as a permanent ongoing concern where realized profits and remitted dividends are more material factors. Long-range implications of rate movements on investment or profit streams will be of more concern than short-term bookkeeping effects. Where the conservation of assets is predominant, realized gains/losses and operating effects will outweigh the possible reporting alterations, and exchange risk management will be carried out accordingly. This approach to foreign exchange risk falls under the concept of 'economic exposure', which takes in all actual effects of parity changes.

In either case, the approach to exchange risk must be (i) organized, (ii) structural and (iii) an integral part of the overall financial management of the firm. The international monetary system remains highly volatile and relationships among currencies are increasingly difficult to predict in the short run. This uncertainty and the exposure risks engendered by rate changes greatly complicate the fragmentation of the international firm.

Multinational companies must now weigh the foreign exchange risk element in each major decision area: the management of liquidity and borrowing, the reporting of financial status, the declaration or repatriation of dividends, and the long-term direct investment decision. No longer can any of these be looked at in isolation. Financing decisions are affected directly by the appreciation or depreciation of the borrower's currency or that which is borrowed; the nominal interest rate alone is only part of the decision-making analysis. The timing of dividends requires an exchange rate judgment to be made and also falls into the overall strategy of dealing with exchange risk. The investment decision itself, normally considered to be based on productivity, market and economic factors, now will include at least a perception of long-term exchange risk. Equivalent investments in two countries, both otherwise offering the same apparent advantages, can be differentiated, and thus graded, by the long-term outlook for the two currencies involved.

If financial management is seen to have as its main objectives the financing and funding of the firm and the protection and efficient utilization of its assets while playing an important role in the planning function, then foreign exchange risk management in the multinational firm is one of its more critical components. This area of management deals with accounting considerations, the safeguarding of stockholder interests, anticipation of future trends in currency movements and the development of a strategy to protect the firm in an uncertain environment. Both short-term and long-term perspectives are involved. The former derives from the immediate problem of protecting the firm's assets and liabilities in all currencies, as well as the current period income, against adverse rate changes. A longer-term horizon deals with the whole planning area of the firm, where financial management must be integrated with sales and production functions, with the long-term financial structure of the firm, with investment planning and with personnel considerations. This is further complicated by the split between accounting/controllership responsibility for reporting and evaluating exchange movements and the treasury's responsibility to anticipate such events while optimizing the use of liquidity in the firm.

Many firms are not yet adequately equipped to approach the exchange risk area. Foreign exchange management requires internal definition and identification of the firm's exchange exposure as a starting point, a number of international companies are still dealing on the basis of incomplete or delayed information. The problem of accounting for exposure, or exchange gains and losses, is itself confused by the traditional freedom allowed by the accounting profession in reporting conventions. Until 1975, for example, U.S. firms were free to consolidate their financial statements in very widely different ways, and to create reserves which could obscure the current impact of rate changes. Firms of many other nationalities still retain this flexibility.

The field of exposure managment, however, can be seen as a logical and structured one. It is sequential, yet interlocking with the other elements of financial management. The object of this book is to show that exchange risks *can* be managed by developing an integrated and anticipatory approach, based on a perception of future flows and positions as well as of present risks. The outline of the book follows closely the structure of exposure management considered appropriate to the international company, shown in Figure 1.

Understanding of exchange risk and the development of a definition of risk for any company begin with the accounting conventions it uses to bring its international transactions to a common basis. These conventions are set by law or by the official accounting body of each

Figure 1. Main components of exposure management

I	II	III
Definition of exposure	Identification of present and projected exposed positions	Analysis of potential impact
(a) That based on accounting rules (b) That risk which goes beyond accounting measurements, particularly local operating effects (economic exposure)	(a) Reporting systems: — internal positions — external data (b) Forecasting systems	(a) Effect of forecast exchange rate movement on corporate positions

IV	V	VI
Strategy setting	Integration with financial management	Tactics for implementing strategy
(a) Cost/risk analysis (b) Use of mathematical tools	(a) Coordination with liquidity management (b) Tax considerations (c) Personnel implications	(a) Selection of hedging techniques: — internal — external (b) Regulatory limitations

country; the rules and practices of the country where the parent is located will predominantly shape its own translation and reporting methods. The accounting background to exchange risk management is therefore set out in Chapter 2.

Again, the accounting effect of foreign exchange exposure is only part of the real exchange risk faced by international companies. Actual transactions in foreign currency on a realized basis present different operating effects at all levels of the company and in future time periods; these may or may not be shown in traditional accounting statements. Additional definition and reporting elements are often necessary to identify these economic risks, which are detailed in Chapter 3.

Proper identification of risk has to be based on reporting systems which attempt to quantify changes in the company's positions over time and to set parameters for the range of exchange risks thereby engendered; this is the subject of Chapter 4. The subsequent chapter gives a model information system to deal with foreign exchange risk which can be adapted to most companies' needs.

Reporting/control systems are at the heart of the identi-fication/analytical process, systems which also identify the external constraints on company response. Only after the future projection of all types of exposure is achieved can the potential impact on a firm and its constituent parts be quantified. Only then can a company develop a strategy to eliminate, reduce or accept its perceived risks. This will normally be decided by its basic attitude to risk, the degree to which any negative results must be publicly reported and the actual after-tax effects if the worst possible set of events happens. The company will review its position currency by currency to achieve this strategy setting, which may often result in a decision to cover all exposed positions where possible in turbulent periods, but to leave certain ones open in more stable times. The assessment of the potential impact of exchange exposure on any company, as the next management stage, is discussed in Chapter 6.

Implementation of the hedging decision is not limited to the use of forward exchange contracts. Many other risk-avoidance or risk-shifting possibilities are open to the multinational firm. Chapter 7 reviews the *internal* techniques which apply to existing exchange positions and those which allow future positions to be modified before losses are incurred. The latter deal with alterations of intercompany payment terms and currencies, with balance sheet adjustments and, in isolated, more radical cases, with changes in a company's financial structure.

The financial markets offer a range of *external* hedging techniques, most of which have a fixed and known cost; these are reviewed in Chapter 8. The combination of both internal and external measures provides the ultimate tactical implementation of the strategy accepted by any one company; both, viewed also from the fiscal implications, should be given equal analysis and be equally understood.

All of these stages are informational and analytical, leading to an active strategy of accepting or covering individual risks. This must be decided by the individual firm from its idiosyncratic factors of stockholder composition, attitude to risk, profit margins and competition. While no precise guidelines can be formulated for this process, Chapter 9 outlines the cost/risk analysis which is at the heart of the process.

Organizing the coordination of these areas goes beyond the technical approach to better information and detailed projections. A way to control and optimize first the decision-making process, and secondly its implementation, must be evolved. Since only a central point can see all types of risks and responses, a strong bias towards centralization is part of a cogent management strategy. Chapter 10 describes three companies' approaches to exchange exposure management as an indication of the implications of centralization, decentralization or doing nothing at all. These cases are complemented by shorter examples throughout the book, reflecting experiences and problems of a wide range of companies.

Mathematical procedures, particularly the use of computers, can be applied to portions of exposure management since one is dealing here with uncertainty and a large number of variables. Among other advantages, the speed and cost factors in data processing allow very rapid and efficient processing of masses of data; exposure identification is particularly fostered. Simulation and optimization models are potential tools to be used in decision making in this area, and the theoretical or mathematical framework is being developed. However, the necessary input for rate predictions is not adequate at present, which has so far hampered these attempts, as shown in Chapter 11.

While foreign exchange exposure management is at the core of the international firm, it is only a portion of its financial management and must be carefully integrated with financial and tax planning. The foreign exchange decision in all the areas outlined above directly impinges upon the financing decision. A major emphasis in the text is thus the interaction of foreign exchange strategy with financing and tax decisions. Normally, all three functions will converge and be mutually worked out at treasurer/finance director levels. Chapters 12 and 13 cover the coordination of these areas.

Lastly, an international company is obviously not dealing here with numbers and control systems alone, but with its personnel abroad and also a range of institutional officials from governments, central banks and commercial banks. The personnel implications of exchange exposure management are reviewed in a final chapter, specifically as they affect the policy of centralizing hedging strategy.

In summary, this volume attempts to give answers or guidelines to the following questions:

(a) How does a firm define the nature of its exposure risk?
(b) How can all types and locations of exchange exposure be identified, both currently and in anticipation of future events?
(c) What reporting systems are necessary for all parts of the exchange exposure management process?
(d) What guidelines are available to understand market trends?
(e) How can a coherent hedging strategy be developed?
(f) How should that strategy be integrated with other financial and tax policies?
(g) How should the firm organize itself internally to deal with this area, and what personnel considerations arise?

The book is directed towards the problems of industrial companies or those providing international services. It does not take into account the unique position of financial institutions, which themselves deal directly in foreign currency. It is meant both as a synthesis of one specific management area and as a general guide to solving the problems of any of its component parts. If these can be more logically approached, the chance of risk minimization can be improved. The ultimate goal is to reduce the impact of the fragmentation which characterizes the international firm.

Implicit in the book is a belief that turbulence in world financial markets will continue, that there will be no quick return to a fixed rate, predictable foreign exchange system, and that exchange control and other barriers are more likely to increase than to decrease. As a result, the exchange exposure management framework outlined in this study requires a policy of centralization and a movement away from the accounting bias of many companies. The effort will usually require modification, if not expansion, of reporting systems and reordering of treasury department responsibilities. Above all, the book suggests a more structured framework for what has sometimes been a neglected field and which has grown in importance to equal more traditional finance functions.

Note
1. There is some basis for the latter concern. See Franck, Peter and Young, Allan, 'Stock price reaction of multinational firms to exchange realignments', *Financial Management*, Winter 1972.

CHAPTER 2

The Accounting Background

The starting point for understanding and managing exchange exposure lies in the accounting methods used to 'translate' balance sheet items and income denominated in different currencies into a single common unit of measurement. Since currencies are constantly changing their value in relation to each other, the underlying transactions, whether realized or pending, need to be recorded in a consistent fashion.

Exchange exposure in the narrowest sense arises from the necessity to portray the company or the group on a single currency basis under constant methods. The different way in which the accounting profession in each country has approached this categorizing and measuring process has resulted in a number of accepted translation conventions. As in other financial spheres, there have been wide variances in the ways companies are allowed to record their foreign currency transactions and to report the resultant effects of rate changes. These conventions differ not only from country to country, but even between similar firms in one country.

The convention used by a particular company determines the basis for management of its accounting exposure. The specific requirements of its accounting conventions will prescribe the ways in which the treasury measures exchange risks and will limit the methods which can be used to deal with them. The effect of these constraints is not always generally understood. They vary from country to country, although the accounting practice of the parent company will ultimately set the framework for the whole group. This chapter delineates the accounting background to exchange risk and the main accounting conventions to elucidate their importance.

An individual firm, of course, cannot change its accounting practices here from time to time, as it might do in inventory evaluation methods or flowing through an investment tax credit. In countries where disclosure and publication of financial statements are mandatory, it must also explain its translation methods. Even so, important discrepancies do result between similar firms using opposing conventions. This asymmetry can lead to misunderstanding by management, by stockholders or analysts. False comparisons could be drawn between indigenous firms in the same industry, or between those in different countries.

Management could be misled about the relative profitability of foreign operations. The treasurer concerned about his company's published results and resultant market appraisal must understand both that effect and the means at his disposal to change it.[1]

Accounting practices relate both to actual trade transactions where settlement brings a realized gain or loss and to consolidation of accounts denominated in foreign currencies. The 'translation' of foreign currency items — restating them arithmetically in terms of a single base currency — can bring unrealized bookkeeping gains or losses. The distinction between unrealized and realized effects has important tax implications, which are reviewed below and in Chapter 13.

Accounting for Realized Losses/Gains

Realized gains or losses arise when a foreign currency is received or paid at a rate different from that at which it was booked, resulting in a greater or smaller amount of domestic currency being received or paid than was originally recorded.

For example, an American importer may order goods from a Swiss supplier at a cost of SF20,000. The goods are received on February 1st when the exchange rate is $1 = SF2.50. If brought on credit, the transaction will be recorded as

Dr.	Inventory	$8000	
	Cr. Liability to Swiss		
	supplier (SF20,000)		$8000

By the end of March, the Swiss franc strengthens against the U.S. dollar to SF2.35. It then requires $8510 to purchase SF20,000. This exceeds the recorded debt by $510, which until payment, is an unrealized loss. On April 2nd, the importer settles its commitment at the new rate, providing $8510 to its bank for the Swiss franc amount sent to the supplier. This is recorded as

Dr.	Liability to Swiss supplier	$8510	
	Cr. Cash		$8510
Debit balance in payable account thus =		$510	
(exchange adjustment)			

The exchange difference caused by the appreciation of the Swiss franc becomes a realized loss at this point, which can be offset against corporate income tax in most cases.

These cases of unrealized and realized losses are straightforward. The unrealized nature of the loss comes from the pending nature of a credit sale; the loss is then realized upon settlement or conversion of the foreign currency amount.

Unrealized losses on translation take a different form, since there will often be no actual settlement or conversion. The following section depicts the three principal translation methods as a background to a situation which has changed or is under scrutiny in many countries. Examples A, B and C show the accounting effects of translating the same subsidiary's balance sheet in three different ways.

Common Conventions in Use for Balance Sheet Consolidation

In the U.S. and Western Europe, three main accounting conventions for the translation of accounts to a common currency have arisen:

Current rate (also called closing rate method);
Current/non-current (working capital method);
Monetary/non-monetary (historic rate method).

Current Rate Method

An obvious means to bring all balance sheet accounts in a multi-national group to a common basis, i.e. the currency in which the parent company reports, is to translate all foreign currency items at the spot rate as of the balance sheet closing date. This method was used by some 90% of U.K. companies, as shown in the latest survey of company accounts published by the Institute of Chartered Accountants,[2] by many firms on the Continent and in the Commonwealth, but by few U.S. multinationals. The philosophy underlying this approach is to take the whole foreign asset/liability structure of the group abroad and consider it, if not at risk, then to be translated in a uniform fashion, whether or not one is dealing with quick assets, fixed plant or long-term debt. As a result, only the net equity of each subsidiary is really exposed, as well as foreign currency commitments of the parent itself.

Since the parent's equity in foreign subsidiaries is by necessity positive (except in rare cases of those in a loss carry-forward position), companies using this method will be 'long' in each currency. When the parent company's currency is depreciating against most others, as the pound sterling has been for several years, there are usually persistent exchange gains to be reported under this method. If the foreign currency has devalued against that of the parent, there is a net loss, shown in Example A.

The closing rate method has strong advocates, who point out that the basic investment of the parent company, i.e. its equity, is translated at the current rate. Fixed assets reflect current earning power, rather than historical cost. The convention is easy to understand and to apply in practice.

However, despite these advantages and its common usage in the English speaking world, this method appears increasingly artificial. Many observers, both accountants and finance managers, do not agree

Example A

A foreign subsidiary to be consolidated into a U.S. parent balance sheet has the following balance sheet at closing date.

	Local Currency
Cash and accounts receivable	800
Inventory	900
Fixed assets (net)	700
Total assets	2400
Current liabilities	900
Long-term debt	500
Net worth	1000
Total liabilities and net worth	2400

These items were booked when LC = $1; by the balance sheet closing date, depreciation of the local currency has brought its value to LC = $0.80. All assets and liabilities are translated at $0.80, so that its balance sheet can be restated in U.S. dollar terms as

Total assets	$1920
Liabilities	1120
Net worth	800

The devaluation has brought a net exchange adjustment of ($200) in the net worth of the subsidiary in dollar terms ($1000–800), which will be reported as a loss.

that the exchange risk inherent in holding cash or short-term investments abroad represents the same sort of risk as fixed assets. Nor is short-term debt of a subsidiary, payable in the near future, comparable to the long-term foreign currency debt or bond issues which may have been placed to buy fixed plant. To translate assets of all types at the closing rate diverges from other traditional accounting concepts relating to actual cost and value. This method, therefore, could be seen to have attractions mainly because of long historical usage and basic simplicity.

Working Capital Method (Current/non-current)

A common translation method in the U.S., although less used abroad, has been to base the translation of assets and liabilities on their short-term or long-term nature. The normal division is one year; assets and liabilities to be received or paid within the year, or the working capital of an affiliate, are translated at the closing spot rate and are therefore susceptible to change in terms of the parent currency. Long-term items — chiefly fixed assets or long-term debt, and financial charges such as depreciation arising from these items — are translated at their historical rates of booking. In the case of the parent itself, the same breakdown applies: working capital items are translated at closing rates, others at historical rates.

Example B

Taking the same subsidiary balance sheet of Example A, different items will be translated at the new rate.

	Local Currency	Items to be adjusted for rate change
Cash and accounts receivable	800	800
Inventory	900	900
Fixed assets	700	
Total assets	2400	1700
Current liabilities	900	900
Long-term debt	500	
Net worth	1000	
Total liabilities and net worth	2400	900

There will be a loss on translation of foreign currency
   assets of 1700 x 0.20   (340)
and a gain on translation of foreign currency liabilities
   of 900 x 0.20   180

The net exchange loss to be reported by the parent
   becomes $(160)

(This can also be calculated by translating the net working capital positions at the new rate: 900 — 1700 x 1.00 — 0.80 = (160).)

This practice brings a more judgmental approach to the reporting of exchange risk positions. The argument here is that the short-term items held or owed by a company (or subsidiary abroad) are subject to rate fluctuation, whereas its fixed plant is not. Certainly the former represent a type of risk more consonant with the short-term relationships between currencies. Long-term debt, to be repaid at some date in the future, is not translated in its entirety at the closing rate under this convention but only the current position due within the year. (This of course does not imply that there is a bigger risk in the one-year portion, but it gives guidance to the treasurer as to the reporting effect of his positions and the actions he may take to adjust them.)

There are fallacies in the working capital method, too, although it was recommended by the American Institute of CPA's Committee on Accounting Procedure in Accounting Research Bulletin, No. 43. This bulletin provided the main guideline for exposure accounting in the U.S. until the changes recommended by the Financial Accounting Standards Board successor to the Accounting Principles Board. Above all, it includes inventory, the traditional valuation of which is cost or market, as an exposed item, but not debt over one year. The confusion arising from this convention has led many U.S. companies to change to the third possibility: the monetary/non-monetary framework.

Monetary/Non-monetary Method

This convention is based on the division of assets and liabilities as to their nature: financial or physical, rather than their maturity. Physical assets, whether short-term (inventory) or long-term (plant and equipment), are translated at their historical rates, with inventory written down to cost or market as relevant. These represent no accounting exchange risk to the parent company, no matter where held or in which currency they were first purchased.

All monetary items, i.e. those denominated in financial terms, are converted at the spot rates pertaining at balance sheet closing. The important difference here, and often the largest single component of exposure, is the translation of long-term debt at the current spot rate. This can create very large book losses, both when the debt is held by the parent, or when it is owed by a subsidiary consolidated in the parent's statements, when the parent's currency depreciates. Such exchange losses have been reported in the early 1970s by U.S. (and to a lesser degree by U.K.) companies with massive Deutsche mark or Swiss franc loans. The converse effect will be shown if the parent currency appreciates.

Example C

	Local Currency	Monetary/non-monetary method accounts to be adjusted
Cash and accounts receivable	800	800
Inventory	900	
Fixed assets	700	
Total assets	2400	800
Current liabilities	900	900
Long-term debt	500	500
Net worth	1000	
Total liabilities and net worth	2400	1400

Here there is a loss on translation of the subsidiary's cash and receivables of (800 x 0.20)	(160)
but a gain on translation of its current and long-term liabilities of (900 + 500 x 0.20)	280
or a net gain/exchange adjustment of	$120

There are many reasons to regard this particular method as coming closest to the other traditions of accountancy and as having the most logical internal framework. While the effects of future spot rate changes on long-term debt cannot and should not be estimated, this convention does call for measurement in present terms at the rate known, i.e. that of the closing date.

This convention, however, does tend to increase sharply the accounting exposure borne by companies which have a higher proportion of long-term debt denominated in foreign currency. These will show poorer financial results in any one period than companies borrowing in their own currency, in times of depreciation of that currency. It may not be possible, or it may be prohibitively expensive, to cover the outstanding risk. The Annual Reports of many companies show such effects.

Unfortunately, there are as yet no adequate ways to weigh all aspects of the treasurer's performance in this area. The 'snap-shot' negative effect of translating debt cannot be offset by the unreported positive effect of having a lower interest cost during the life of the loan, which may in certain cases outweigh the effect of debt revaluation. The treasurer may decide to borrow Deutsche marks at a cost of 5% when long-term loans in his own currency would bear a rate of 10%. The discounted cash flow effect of a 5% interest differential over the life of the loan may be lower than the loss involved when the mark appreciates against the base currency and capital and interest payments increase. The result, of course, depends on the timing and extent of that appreciation.

While the monetary/non-monetary method appears to be the most appropriate way to portray a company's accounting exposure in today's markets, certain objections have been raised to its use, mainly in the classification of items into strictly monetary or otherwise. Some assets or liabilities may have both characteristics, such as debt instruments. Inventory is a controversial item here, as in other conventions. Some companies feel that inventory, which is steadily replenished, is as exposed as any other working capital item. Although the monetary/ non-monetary convention may be used, inventory is then translated at the closing rate as well. The elasticity of demand for inventory held internationally can also be important for risk management, as rate changes in the currency in which inventory will be sold will affect sales accordingly. (This touches on the subject of economic exposure, which goes beyond accounting techniques and is reviewed in more detail in Chapter 3.) Long-term investments held in the form of marketable securities could also be translated either at historical cost or at the market value at closing date.

Translation of Income

Income translation is circumscribed by more readily agreed-upon principles. The determinant factor is the percentage share held of a subsidiary to be consolidated. Under U.S. practice, if more than 50% of a foreign affiliate is owned directly, its entire income for the accounting period (and its non-intercompany balance sheet items) is consolidated.

If 20—50% is owned, the proportionate share is brought into the parent's profit and loss statement. If holdings in subsidiaries fall below that percentage, they may be carried solely as an investment, and any income to be considered would be in the form of declared dividends. Branch income is considered fully that of the parent. U.K. rules are similar.

Income is normally accrued over the year and translated at average rates during the period. This is often done at month-end values for the preceding month, which gives an acceptable approximation. Internally, standard booking rates will be applied for daily transactions, which are then adjusted to the actual rates at closing dates. A problem can arise if companies allow these internal rates to get too far out of line from those pertaining in the markets, particularly between quarterly reports and the final accounting for the year.

Reserve Creation

To compensate for financial disclosure requirements, a number of companies have established reserves for foreign operations, or more stringently, for foreign exchange gains and losses. Reserves of U.S. companies have to be reported as to amount, together with activity in the reserve and the full policy in regard to translation. The ways in which reserves are created, and the detail of disclosure, still vary from company to company and this also has been an area of possible confusion and even obfuscation. Where discrepancies, both in accounting convention and reserves, appear, one can readily see that both objective reporting to the outside world and understanding are impaired.

Common statements such as the following appear in many annual reports.

'As in prior years, the net realized exchange adjustments arising from translation have been charged or credited to the Reserve for Foreign Operations which was established for this purpose. Realized exchange adjustments are charged or credited to income.'

Such a statement tells little to the outside world, whereas quantified descriptions of reserve creation do:

'Net translation gains of $5,635,000 at September 29th, 1973 (including $3,406,000 arising in 1973) were reserved in current liabilities and after $1,000,000 amortization in 1974, net translation losses of $1,564,000 at September 28th, 1974, were included in deferred charges.'

Similarly:

'Because of uncertainties and fluctuations in world monetary conditions, in 1973 approximately $1,300,000 of net unrealized gains from translation were deferred until the related net assets are converted into U.S. dollars.'

The temptation to use the freedom in translation and reserve practice to show one's company in the best light must have been strong in financial history. In one of the more radical cases, one U.S. company created a reserve which was credited with the opportunity costs saved by not hedging foreign risks. The Board of Directors of that company allowed its treasury department to remain uncovered on any risks which would not cost the parent more than $0.10 per share after taxes, according to their best estimates. This allowed a more aggressive policy of remaining uncovered; aggregate credits to the reserve in six figures ensued. As the dollar weakened, losses were matched against the reserve and reported only on a net basis to the public.

Much could be said in favour of a liberal, if standardized, reserve policy. Among other things, it would allow a more equitable judgment of all facets of the treasury decision as in the lower cost of borrowing/debt appreciation case. Foreign exchange reserves for U.S. industrial corporations, however, are now a thing of the past, due to the new Financial Accounting Standards Board (FASB) Statement No. 8, published in October 1975.

FASB Rationalization of U.S. Accounting Practice

The Financial Accounting Standards Board put an end to the discrepancies and confusion caused by different translation and reserve methods in the U.S. by this announcement. In 1974/5 it went through a short but intensive study of the question, soliciting the help and opinions of the U.S. business community through its Discussion Memorandum 'Accounting for Foreign Currency Translation' and the Exposure Draft dated December 31st, 1974. The latter gave the outlines of the present practice; since it is also an outstanding portrayal of the arguments and counter-arguments for each type of accounting approach, part of the Exposure Draft is attached as an Appendix. The definitive convention for U.S. companies was then published as Statement of Financial Accounting Standards No. 8. 'Accounting for the Translation of Foreign Currency Transactions and Foreign Currency Financial Statements.'

The Board was concerned that the major discrepancies — intentional or otherwise — in U.S. accounting practice in this area be eliminated, and that the most suitable method be prescribed. The result was the *temporal* method of translation of accounts, which had the following major new requirements for U.S. companies:

(a) All U.S. non-financial companies must follow one standard practice in accounting for foreign exchange transactions, and in group consolidation.

(b) Reserves to shift the impact of exchange gains or losses into different time periods are not permitted.

(c) Forward contracts of companies hedging currency risks must be valued at closing date, and their accrued loss or gain taken into period income, except for forward contracts which exactly cover, in magnitude, currency and tenor, transactional commitments in foreign currency.

These are major changes. For fiscal years beginning on or after January 1st, 1976, all U.S. companies must follow the temporal convention, or lack certification of their financial statements by their outside auditors. No room for hiding gains or losses under loosely-constructed reserves is available.

The recording of profits and/or losses on unrealized forward exchange contracts is the most important departure from tradition. These are off-balance sheet items which have neither been evaluated nor reported publicly. The Board, however, insisted that there can be a substantive risk, or financial change, in such commitments over time which should be taken into account.

Specifically, it requires that gains or losses on outstanding forward exchange contracts pertaining to (a) a hedge of an exposed net asset or liability position, (b) speculation or (c) a hedge of a foreign currency commitment not meeting the conditions described above, be included in the determination of current income. Forward contracts are also seen as individual transactions, to be accounted for openly and separately from the original transaction or position they are covering.

When practical, past financial results were recommended to be restated to conform to the new provisions of Statement No. 8, rather than reported as a one-time adjustment to earnings, which would have fostered some very massive swings for certain companies.

Basic Rules of the 'Temporal' Convention

The newly prescribed accounting convention differs only slightly in practice from the earlier monetary/non-monetary translation technique. It is still based upon the division of balance sheet items as to their basic temporality. Items which are carried at prices in past exchanges (past prices) are to be translated at historical rates. Accounts carried at prices in current purchase or sale exchanges (current prices) or future exchange (future prices) are translated at the closing spot rate.

Inventory is still a special case. If the rule of cost or market, whichever is lower, is used, the company should compare translated historical cost with translated market. If already written down to market, it is translated at the spot rate of the date of writedown.

A schemata of the rule regarding each major balance sheet item is given in Figure 2.

Figure 2. Rates used to translate assets and liabilities under the temporal method

	Translation rates	
	Current	Historical
Assets		
Cash on hand, demand and time deposits	X	
Marketable securities		
Carried at cost		X
Carried at current market price	X	
Accounts and notes receivable	X	
Allowance for doubtful accounts and notes receivable	X	
Inventories		
Carried at cost		X
Carried at current replacement or current selling price	X	
Carried at net realizable value	X	
Carried at contract price (produced under fixed-price contracts)	X	
Pre-paid insurance, advertising, rent and other pre-payments		X
Investments in unconsolidated subsidiaries or other investees carried at cost		X
Property, plant and equipment		X
Accumulated depreciation of property, plant and equipment		X
Deferred income tax charges		X
Patents, trademarks, licences, formulae		X
Goodwill		X
Other intangible assets and deferred charges		X
Liabilities		
Accounts and notes payable	X	
Accrued expenses payable	X	
Deferred income		X
Bonds payable or other long-term debt	X	
Unamortized premium or discount and pre-paid interest on bonds or notes payable	X	
Convertible bonds payable	X	
Accrued pension obligations	X	
Obligations under warranties	X	
Deferred income tax credits		X

Other Countries' Attempts to Standardize Foreign Exchange Accounting

United Kingdom

In the U.K. the rule-making body is the Accounting Standards

Steering Committee (ASSC) of the Institute of Chartered Accountants in England and Wales in association with its sister Institutes in the U.K. ASSC accounting procedures are binding in the form of 'Statements of Standard Accounting Practice.' No definitive 'statement' on the subject of accounting for foreign currency items has appeared. The Institute itself begs the question by stating in its official recommendations: 'The fundamental uncertainties involved in exchange operations make it impossible to lay down hard and fast rules for conversion into sterling of the accounts of overseas branches and subsidiaries and emphasize the need for each case to be judged on its merits in light of particular circumstances . . . In normal circumstances, both the "historic rate" and "closing rate" methods are widely used and equally acceptable in practice.'[3]

However, the ASSC published an Exposure Draft on 'Extraordinary Items and Prior Year Adjustments' in September 1975, which touches upon 'Foreign Currency Translation'. It proposes that exchange differences be dealt with directly through the profit and loss accounts, and that they be treated as extraordinary items only if arising from transactions themselves coming under that definition. Exchange differences on translation of fixed asset amounts (arising from the use of the closing rate method) are proposed to be treated as if they were unrealized surpluses or deficits on revaluation of fixed assets and dealt with through reserves.

The U.K. accounting profession is, at the time of writing, engrossed in the implications of current cost accounting as developed in the Sandilands Report. This may delay the adoption of a single standard for U.K. practice in foreign currency translation, although a further exposure draft on this subject is expected in 1976.

A growing feeling is that U.S. changes will eventually reverberate and cause similar moves in the U.K. to a more realistic, temporally-based convention.[4] As stated above, the closing rate method is predominant, perhaps because U.K. companies originally viewed their foreign investments in terms of return on equity. Those using the 'historic rate' method, according to the ICA, were influenced by a pattern of largely financing and stocking foreign subsidiaries directly from the U.K.

Continental Europe

The range of translation conventions permitted in the U.K., and until recently in the U.S., is also found on the Continent. Here also, companies in many countries do not have to consolidate subsidiaries into the parent balance sheet or to report fully in the Anglo-Saxon manner. All companies, of course, will prepare consolidated figures for internal use, and their usual practice is the closing rate method.

An obvious area of harmonization within the EEC itself would be foreign exchange accounting. Tax harmonization, at the time of writing, is receiving more attention and there are few signs of movement towards uniformity of accounting procedures.

The sole progress on a wider scale is the creation of the International Accounting Standards Committee (IASC), established by the accountancy institutes of nine founding countries (Australia, Canada, France, Germany, Japan, Mexico, the Netherlands, the U.K. and Ireland, and the U.S.) to formulate basic international accounting standards. Only one standard, on the principle of disclosure of accounting conventions, has so far appeared, and it did not attempt to set any guidelines for exposure accounting. On the other hand, a large number of other countries have begun to associate themselves with the IASC and it has been endorsed by the International Federation of Stock Exchanges.[5]

Differences Between Accounting Conventions and Fiscal Reporting

It should be noted parenthetically that the foreign exchange gains and losses reported under any of these accounting methods will not usually give rise to tax considerations, except for realized gains and losses emanating from completed transactions and conversions taken into gross income.

Publicly reported gains or losses on translation will not correspond with calculation of taxable income or assist in tax strategy since they normally have no fiscal significance. Conversely, negative operating or liquidity effects, particularly those likely to be suffered in future periods after rate changes, may not be picked up by any of the accounting conventions presently in use. These are discussed at length in Chapter 3.

The dichotomy between realized and unrealized effects, and between accounting and economic exposure, raises a number of problems for financial executives in determining all types of exchange risk. Identifying both accounting and economic exposure leads to the heart of the area: determining what should be hedged and by what means, which forms the bulk of this volume.

Notes

1. This point is developed in more detail in S. C. Peterson, 'Impact of accounting methods on foreign exchange management', *Euromoney*, June 1974. He is Assistant Treasurer, American Standard.
2. *Institute of Chartered Accountants*. Survey of Published Accounts 1973/4, London, 1975.
3. *Institute of Chartered Accountants*. Recommendations on Accounting Principles, London, 1975 edition; pp108—9.
4. Flower, J. F., 'Coping with currency fluctuations in company accounts', *Euromoney*, June 1974.
5. *Financial Times*, July 15, 1975.

CHAPTER 3

Economic Exposure

The previous chapter presented the variegated accounting background to the exposure management problem. However, analysis of standard financial statements *per se* does not provide an answer to the question 'What is actually exposed in any one company?' The answer is the key to the framework of risk management for the specific firm. Its accounting exposure risk has already been defined as the possibility that published financial statements will show a negative impact from currency movements. This definition, however prevalent in shaping companies' attitudes to exchange exposure, is insufficient for total understanding of exchange exposure. Accounting information does not show all of the effects which currency rate changes have on a company, but only those which change current period income in measuring the value of its assets and liabilities and its income statement components.

Exposure management based on accounting considerations is by necessity static and historically oriented. By definition, it does not look to the future effects of parity changes which have occurred or may possibly occur in the future.

These effects may be seen in the short term on a company's liquidity or later in its entire operations, financial structure and profits. The whole range of such risks is defined as *economic exposure*. This type of exposure emanates from those positions where an actual conversion will be made or where the cash flow effect of an exchange loss is an impediment to the operations of one subsidiary. It can arise in the impact on future sales of a company situated in a country whose currency has appreciated, or on future profits where the local currency has depreciated, even putting the viability of a subsidiary into question.

The impact of actual conversions is commonly called 'transaction exposure', but this is not as all-encompassing as the term 'economic exposure'. Later sections of this chapter show a number of examples of economically exposed situations and their distinction from accounting exposure. Once again, the importance of this additional exposure element, not always perceived by international firms, is the necessity to understand it and fit those additional risks into a system of anticipatory management.

The word 'exposure' itself is of course neutral, simply signifying that the company has assets or liabilities, or income streams, denominated in currencies other than its own. Changes in the foreign currencies involved may be positive. The 'risk' in such exposure is that such changes bring negative results, again either in accounting or real terms; effects of the latter sort may develop only in the future. Exchange risk should be seen as including both possibilities and a system to identify, analyse and control all types of exposure risk should be the goal of finance management.

Economic Exposure — Short-term

A multinational company lends its parent currency, say dollars, to a subsidiary in the U.K. This loan will not be included in accounting exposure, as (i) such intercompany accounts are excluded in consolidation, and (ii) it is denominated in the currency in which the balance sheet is consolidated.

To the subsidiary, this represents an economic exposure which could have serious operating effects if the pound depreciates against the dollar. If the amount of the loan is $1,000,000 and it is made at a point when £1 = $2.40, the subsidiary will book its debt as £416,667. Over the life of the loan, the pound may depreciate to $2.00. The subsidiary will have to furnish £500,000 to repay the $1,000,000 capital amount and bears a realized loss of £83,333. If large transactions relative to its size are involved, the cash losses may impair its liquidity. In extreme cases, the subsidiary could already be at the limit of its borrowing facilities during a, time of severe credit restriction. It may not be possible to increase its local borrowings to produce the increased debt repayment, which means that its working capital ratios suffer, i.e. payables must be extended or inventory run down. Higher costs or operational difficulties result.

Another example is the local cash holdings of a foreign subsidiary. A subsidiary in Italy may maintain a cash/short-term investment account of $1,000,000 equivalent in lire. From the group's accounting point of view, this represents part of the lire exposure which will affect the group's balance sheet if the base currency appreciates against the lire. The subsidiary will have no accounting exposure, since this is its own local currency. If its operations are carried out solely in Italy and it has no foreign currency commitments, it will bear no short-term economic loss no matter what the lira may do. The accounting risk could be seen as totally artificial as related to a permanent, ongoing subsidiary. If, however, it has built up the lire cash position in anticipation of dividends or future import payments, it will bear an economic risk. (This is further verified if the parent company covers its net lire positions forward by a forward sale. The group then has no accounting exposure; the economic exposure of the subsidiary remains.)

Economic Exposure — Long-range

Future effects of parity changes also arise under the general category of economic risk, and may be of material importance. A subsidiary may have been established in a country with low rates of inflation, readily available funds for borrowing, balance of payments surpluses and low rates of taxation. These factors could have played a part in the decision to establish the subsidiary. Over time, the economic situation of the country deteriorates and those positive features disappear. Eventually, the local currency will devalue or depreciate, either from official action or market forces. The subsidiary may immediately face operating problems if it imports from harder currency sources or if it has borrowed from abroad. Economic factors in its country of operation will also be affected by rate movements. Inflationary forces may change the price structure of a local subsidiary, particularly if imports or raw materials are made much more expensive. Price controls may follow an exchange rate devaluation, local labour availability will react and may be diminished. The supply of loanable funds in the country may be restricted by market forces or official action, so that the subsidiary cannot increase its borrowing facilities when needed. These problems, too, come under economic exposure, as would equivalent ones of a subsidiary whose currency has appreciated and whose exports are eventually reduced as a result.

Accounting reports will pick up none of these problems. It can readily be seen that they affect not only exposure management, but the whole finance and planning function of the firm. Foreign exchange risks of all kinds must be coordinated with planning and budgeting, with the direct investment decision, with debt structure and with liquidity placement. The role of economic exposure makes the need for coordination that much more apparent.

Analysis Needed for Identification of Economic Exposure

To identify economic exposure requires analysis 'beyond the balance sheet'. The nature of each item should be examined beyond the immediate translation level, specifically as to its ultimate impact on each affected entity of the group. This impact is not always represented just as a direct foreign exchange gain or loss. It may have major negative effects on an affiliate's liquidity or need to borrow; it will also have to be analysed as to its fiscal implications. Future sales or income streams need to be brought into the analysis.

A major element in this book is the need to anticipate events and to formulate strategies relating to risk before these occur. This is equally critical at the level of economic exposure as it is in accounting exposure management, since the former is overlooked in traditional reporting systems. It is as important to tie in potential operating effects of exposure with cash and borrowing forecasts as it is to anticipate the changes in financial positions reported publicly.

Economic Exposure in Intercompany Accounts

Perhaps the most common area in which exposure beyond the accounting level arises, and can be underestimated, is in intercompany transactions. In consolidation, intercompany accounts are not directly brought into the parent company balance sheet. For this reason, many companies leave out intercompany positions when reporting exchange exposure to the parent; one often hears the comment 'intercompany accounts aren't exposed' as a justification of this, since one unit's loss is thought to be another unit's gain.

However, intercompany transactions can represent significant operating effects for the local subsidiary, whether they are in the form of loans or trade transactions.

Loans

An example of intercompany loans and the difference between their accounting and economic effects was given above. Many parent companies provide funds to subsidiaries in the form of long-term loans, without considering the effect over time of divergence of the two currencies.

Trade Transactions

An economic effect can be seen in intercompany trade accounts, where a local affiliate must produce more local currency to settle the same level of intergroup payables; these again will usually show no pre-tax effect for the firm on consolidation.

Tax Effects

Economic exposure appears also in the fiscal impact of intercompany transactions. It is not valid to say that it makes no difference which side bears the exchange loss, as the other side picks up an equivalent gain. This is true only if two criteria are met: that both affiliates have roughly the same corporate tax rate, and that the payable/receivable is denominated in one of the currencies of the two locations. (When the latter case is not present, i.e. intercompany trade is denominated in a third currency, there can be a net loss if the currencies move in certain directions.)

The tax effect can be seen in the following experience of a U.S. multinational with subsidiaries in England and Germany. The U.K. affiliate had a massive tax carry forward, thereby having an effective null tax rate. The German subsidiary was prospering and paid the full German corporate tax rate (51% if no dividends were paid out). Both sold a large volume of products to each other and invoiced this trade in their local currency respectively. Over the past several years, the appreciation of the mark relative to the pound created more losses in the U.K. and taxable gains in Germany. If both subsidiaries had been profitable, both paying around 50% tax, the situation would not have been critical. There was a net loss to the group in this case, a type of economic risk arising from the differential tax impact, which can be reduced or eliminated by changing the currency of billing.

Tax differentials are, of course, well-known to, and major considerations of, international firms. They are sometimes treated as a completely separate area from foreign exchange, however, rather than being coordinated so that strategy or tactics aim toward an optimum decision and better financial planning. Chapter 13 shows the importance of integrating both management areas.

Economic Exposure in Inventory

Another balance sheet area not commonly regarded as exposed is inventory. Using the monetary/non-monetary or temporal methods, inventory is not generally treated as an exposed item; under the current/non-current method it is converted at the spot rate in consolidation, but represents an accounting risk only in the local currency in which it is denominated.

Inventory can present economic risks in many cases. If inventory is bought from foreign hard currency sources and sold in local currency, there is an immediate economic effect if the import currency appreciates over time and local prices cannot be raised. Both marketing considerations and often price controls in a depreciating currency country make this a typical situation. Accounting data will normally show only the local currency value and may fail to give management sufficient guidance for a price increase decision.

There may be a world price for certain types of goods, purely local prices for others. In the chemical industry, a number of bulk products have a virtually universal price, to which local subsidiary companies adhere. That price may be quoted in U.S. dollars; as the dollar depreciates, so does the local price.

Economic risks can also be seen in inventory destined to be sold abroad. Although carried in a hard currency, inventory in Germany may represent a high proportion of future export sales to Italy, which will be denominated in lire. The resulting lire receivables represent a much different exposure to the group from the ostensible Deutsche mark inventory, of which the treasurer, if not the group accountant, will again want to be apprised.

Economic exposure in inventory can be identified if the company examines all sourcing and exporting patterns, once more 'looking beyond the balance sheet'. This means projecting the replenishment or turnover in inventory in the future. Some companies have set up elaborate reporting systems to do this; one example of such a report is described in Chapter 5. Other break out their inventory for reporting/control purposes into that which has a world price and that which has a local price.

At a more sophisticated level, companies can try to forecast their sourcing patterns over a longer period of time or analyse the price elasticity of each inventory group to ascertain what price or currency adjustment can be made to respond to expected risk. The timing factor in economic exposure can be seen to be a major one — looking at present positions in the balance sheet and projecting their currency elements forward is its essence.

Expected cash flows are part of the future element in economic exposure. Some firms, for instance, calculate and then hedge the entire net income of affiliates forward for a year, although the sales have not been made and the actual dividend payout rate is uncertain. Their attitude is that this protects the consolidated income statement, no matter what happens in the currency markets. It gives local subsidiaries up to a year to change the local price level or make other adjustments which counteract currency movement. On the other hand, forecasted cash flows themselves can be radically affected by a rate change in the subsidiary's country, making the planning process more difficult.

Economic exposure is an integral part of exchange risk and must be understood, anticipated and integrated into the management systems of international companies. The long-term operational nature of economic risk may create an inherent tension between the goal of minimizing accounting losses and the efforts of management to mitigate the possible negative operating and cash flow results of rate changes over time. For example, the imminent devaluation of a currency might call for large-scale and costly hedging action, but increased investment in the country of that devaluation is likely to create profitable business conditions, particularly for exporters.[1] Other rate developments may depress, even permanently, the profitability of operations in one country.

To take full account of economic exposure requires modification of traditional accounting systems, which often do not pick up operating risks fully and which are historically based. Additional reports and analysis will be required by the treasury which are unnecessary for the controller/accounting department, as shown in the following section. Even closer coordination with liquidity management and tax strategy is necessary; these facets are covered in later chapters. Lastly, a decision must be taken as to the relative importance of accounting and operating effects of rate changes on the firm in order to set a proper strategy to control both.

Note

1. Dufey, Gunter, 'Corporate finance and exchange rate variation' *Financial Management*, Summer 1972, is an excellent portrayal of these conflicts.

CHAPTER 4

Identification of Exchange Exposure,
A: Reporting Elements

The type of reporting system necessary to identify a company's exchange exposure will be shaped by its international structure, attitude to risk and the extent to which its management wishes to control this area actively. Adequate reporting systems range from rudimentary to very complex, depending on individual corporate requirements. While the typical problem is one of insufficient detail and forecasting, it is also possible to demand more information than is needed for good risk management in a single company, with resultant strain on personnel, inefficiency in compilation and unnecessary expense.

A number of international companies have not instituted an adequate or consistent approach to the problem of identifying all types of exchange risk. A detailed, treasury-oriented and *anticipatory* reporting system must be developed before a programme for the reduction or elimination of risk can be contemplated. This chapter provides an outline of the reports necessary to analyse a company's present and projected exposure, to ascertain the potential impact on its financial statements and operations and to determine the constraints imposed on its response to that potential impact. It concludes that exchange risks *are* measurable, if a logical and structured information system is used.

Differing Accounting and Treasury Orientations

Most of the necessary data for such a logical procedure are normally available within the accounting mechanism of the company, but not always specifically oriented towards, or used in conjunction with, exposure management. All international companies have, by necessity, an internal accounting system which presents the financial position of the concern at regular intervals. These reports are used for consolidation, for management control purposes and for publication of financial statements. By their nature, they are historically based and provide a picture of the company at one moment in time. They also tend to be sales- and income-oriented. Normal accounting records, therefore, are of only limited use to the treasurer in determining exchange risk strategy. Specifically, accounting reports may be deficient in:

  detail;
  timeliness;
  distribution;
  anticipation;
  information on economic exposure.

These problems arise from the different orientations of the accounting and treasury sections of a company. The accounting system will be
based on reports where intercompany accounts are left out in consolidation; it may require subsidiary financial statements to be already
translated into the parent currency before submission. Reports may be
quarterly; they may also be concentrated in the accounting section and
just summaries given to the treasury department. Accounting reports
rarely include forecasts (although the separate budgeting process of
course does).

A balanced approach will satisfy the requirements of both accounting and the treasury functions of the firm. The treasury needs to obtain
more data, particularly that which is not included in consolidation.
There must be a differently structured set of reports available to the
treasury department from each entity in the group. As will be shown
later, this presupposes a central control function at treasury level, as the
only point which can thereafter analyse both individual and aggregate
positions of the group and correlate exposures with liquidity and
financing considerations.

This information need can usually be fulfilled without proliferation
of reports. The bulk of contemporary position data is available within
the company; what is often necessary is merely restructuring or
modification of the reporting process. Future position projections by
currency may be more difficult to achieve, but these are related to the
budget data; currency elements may be further interpolated and
projected under the same assumptions, if actual forecasts are not
available.

The identification problem is different for the importing or exporting company from that for the multinational company with foreign
subsidiaries, as the next two sections show.

Reporting in the Export/Import Company

For an exporting or importing concern, parity changes are directly
reflected in its financial statements. Exposure will arise only in certain
assets (accounts receivable, perhaps cash) and certain liabilities (import
payables and foreign currency borrowings). The reporting system
necessary here requires that these items be broken out by amount,
currency and maturity. For export orders received, but not booked,

exporting divisions should prepare estimated sales reports such that the financial manager can take possible increased exposure into account. The same sort of estimation can be used to evaluate exposure risks from unbooked import orders.

This seemingly simple task can be complicated by decentralization of the company. Many export firms have either a multiproduct or multidivisional structure; these usually have decentralized export billing and decentralized purchasing of raw materials. In such companies, line units of manufacturing locations can bill in foreign currency without reporting to the central finance function, or commit the company to foreign currency payments for imports with the same lack of information. As a result, newly created exchange exposure may not be made known to the treasury until month-end, even if line units are dealing under guidelines as to which currencies to accept in sales or purchase contracts. Usually only the amount of new exposure by currency is reported. In the worst cases, marketing units may invoice exports without even the exact currency being known in advance at treasury levels. When such delays or omissions occur in fragile markets, swings in currencies can result in substantial losses before the net position by currency is identified or appropriate action taken. The need for timely, detailed reports, and for close coordination between marketing/purchasing and finance departments is apparent.

Reporting in the Company with Consolidated Subsidiaries

Here the whole range of exposure risk problems appears. The reporting mechanism must serve the purpose of both accounting and financial management. (Actual examples of reporting forms will be found in Chapter 5.) Thus the accounting department will wish to be able to measure the performance of the company worldwide and evaluate its global assets, liabilities and commitments. The treasurer will wish to ascertain which of those positions are exposed to currency risk and what the future trends will be of the company's balance sheet structure and income streams. He will require additional information on these areas along the following lines.

Detail

The critical element in exposure management is to pinpoint as precisely as possible the position of the group in each currency. Local balance sheets must distinguish those items denominated in local currency from those in each specific foreign currency; this is often overlooked. Budget reports should contain a similar breakdown.

Timing

Some companies still consolidate the group balance sheet only quarterly. This is inadequate for the treasurer's perception of risk.

Monthly reporting is essential (and increasingly instituted); where monthly balance sheets are not usually submitted to the parent, a separate report of exposed items may suffice. Given the time involved in balance sheet preparation and mailing, a summary telex 'flash' report of exposed items by currency and other items may be necessary.

Distribution

The data in the reports above should be sent directly to the treasury. Too often accounting/financial data are submitted to the controller with delayed reporting to the treasurer. One U.S. company sends the financial statements of its European subsidiaries first to New York, then to California, where accounting for the international division is carried out. Only after consolidation there are they finally sent back to the treasurer. Since, on the other hand, the treasury department may find it difficult to process or compile all the data input of a large, complex company, controller/accounting department or computer assistance may be required.

Anticipation/Forecasting

Foreign exchange management can only be effective when foreign currency positions at risk are anticipated and their potential impact on the firm analysed. In the multinational company, an attempt must be made to identify changes over time in all currency risks of the group and its subsidiaries. The budgetary procedures of almost all companies do not allow this per se, since they are based on sales or profit expectations. While forecasting is an extraordinarily difficult process, anticipation of individual currency risks is critical. To deal on the basis of current numbers only, themselves certainly days or weeks out of date, means that strategy cannot be properly set. In many instances, companies have believed themselves to be net short or long in a given currency and have responded accordingly. For example, a number of U.S. companies which do not forecast and started a period with a net short position in pounds have allowed that supposed position to remain in anticipation of sterling weakening. In several of these companies, the net short position moved to neutral or long in pounds without the parent being aware soon enough of the changed risk this involved. In the worst of these cases, that swing also corresponded with a depreciation of the pound against the dollar. The overall strategy to remain 'short' in sterling was overtaken by the real, unperceived swing in their positions, with the result that actual and sometimes material losses were suffered, without awareness of this until after the fact. Any tactics used to implement a strategy based on obsolete data could make that problem worse. Despite its difficulty, there are certain methods which lend themselves to forecasting by currency, discussed below.

Compilation of Economic Exposure

To repeat the substance of Chapter 3, the reporting system must also be based on additional, non-accounting data to allow a central control point to understand the effect of exchange risk on all parts of the group. The reports described so far allow the identification of the company's consolidated exposure in accounting terms, i.e. basically those items which have a negative effect in consolidation if the currency in which they are denominated changes in value. Accounting reports which eliminate intercompany positions, of course, inhibit total understanding of the effects of parity changes on any one subsidiary.

Cash forecasts showing anticipated receipts and expenditures of each subsidiary in each currency are necessary. Even though the group shows a neutral position in a particular currency due to hedging, the subsidiary's operating effects will vary greatly depending on the expected disposition of its cash balance. The subsidiary's liquidity may be impaired even if the group has a covered net position, and the parent may not be able to adjust it.

Specific inventory reports may also be appropriate, as analysis shows economic elements at the subsidiary level. Inventory held in a French subsidiary will be seen as a French franc exposure in accounting terms, if at all. That inventory may be sold in a variety of currencies or replenished from hard currency sources; as it moves through the production cycle, the resultant accounts payable or receivable represent quite different exposures.

Certain industries have a split inventory problem, in that part is based on a 'world' price, the remainder on a local price structure. That which has a 'world' price — oil, heavy chemicals — may be considered unexposed at parent company level. The exposure reports, or balance sheet, may in these cases break down inventory into those two groupings, whereas accounting data would not need to have that breakdown for its measurement purposes.

Reporting for Unconsolidated Subsidiaries — MEXICO

For accounting purposes, unconsolidated subsidiaries either have no effect on exposure (i.e. they are carried at historical investment cost) or are consolidated according to their percentage value.

There is little difference in the reporting elements necessary for the treasury level to take into account any exposure risks arising here. If subsidiaries are 20—50% owned, under U.S. and other countries' accounting rules the firm's percentage share of income is taken into group income, and the same percentage of the balance sheet is translated and consolidated in the group's financial statements. In these cases, large subsidiaries' positions may indeed affect the firm's overall exchange risk; this potential impact must be similarly identified. In the area of economic exposure, it can be as important to determine the economic risks of unconsolidated affiliates as to study those of consolidated ones. (Local minority interest, of course, will often make it very difficult to take offsetting reactions to avoid exposures at the subsidiary level. The parent may try to lag payments to the subsidiary, or accelerate payments from it, to reduce a net long position in the relevant currency. Both of these affect its liquidity position and either reduce its interest income or increase interest exposure, to the detriment of the local minority partner.)

The income effect can also be substantial; the process of analysing and forecasting income for large minority-held subsidiaries should be attempted. Since these flows are partially a component of group income, it may become necessary to hedge them or the related dividends, when arising from weak currency sources.

Forecasting Future Positions

No firm will be able to forecast precisely all of its gross positions by currency in the future (although in one case, a large U.S. multinational requires detailed balance sheets broken down by currency, to be forecast monthly by each subsidiary for 13 monthly periods forward). It is important to estimate the magnitude and direction of change in positions, not the exact positions themselves; a quarterly forecast may suffice.

Certain tools lend themselves to the forecasting process.

Ratio Analysis

Depending on the accounting convention used, exposed items will include cash and short-term investments, accounts receivable, inventory, short-term borrowings and accounts payable, or long-term debt. Several of these items are direct functions of sales. Future balance sheet projections, whether prepared manually or by computer, are based on relatively constant ratios of liquidity, receivables and inventory to sales. Two factors are involved; first, analysis of the ratio itself, i.e. will the ratio of X% cash to sales remain stable over time or can it itself vary? The latter may occur if new customer groups are approached, if customers' payment habits deteriorate or different credit terms are offered. Secondly, the application of that ratio and those involving receivables and inventory, after similar examination of ratio constancy, to future sales budgets gives the parameters of those balance sheet items.

To identify the future foreign currency aspects, analysis of the currency components of each balance sheet item is necessary; again a ratio analysis may help. A subsidiary in Germany may show the currency breakdown of Example D in its working capital.

Example D
% Currency breakdown in working capital

Percentage	Deutsche mark	Dollar	Pound	French franc	Other
Cash	95	5	0	0	0
Short-term investment	100	0	0	0	0
Accounts receivable	80	10	2	5	3 (SF)
Accounts payable	40	30	10	10	10 (Hfl)

Analysis of the possible changes in these ratios, when compiled with the projected position in each balance sheet category, gives further definition of the currency risks of such a subsidiary in the future.

Comparison with Liquidity Forecasts

The critical items of cash, short-term investments or borrowings are included in liquidity forecasts. Forecasts should be projected by currency, but in any event are combined with balance sheet/sales ratios in the net currency forecasting procedure. Liquidity changes in ensuing periods may substantially change the resultant group exposure in any currency. For example, a subsidiary of a U.S. parent, whose net working capital position is defined and consolidated as part of group exposure, may have brought its working capital to a neutral point by local borrowing. If it moves over time to a more liquid position from whatever cause: increased profits, better credit management, decreased inventory, thus reducing local sterling borrowings, the net exposure of the group in that currency is correspondingly increased. This should be anticipated by management, for in times of speculative pressure it can become substantially more expensive to cover the increased exposure.

Income Forecasts

Apart from the pure balance sheet analysis, the currency breakdown of future income (and future dividends) is an instrumental part of the ultimate exposure strategy setting. In the simplest form, income streams can be considered as arising solely in the currency of the affiliate in question. The projected future income stream will affect the group income statement if the currency it is achieved in depreciates over the year (income being translated at average, usually month-end, rates). The finance department may wish to take measures to protect income by internal measures (price adjustments, etc.) or to cover it forward. Dividends are virtually always declared and paid in the currency of the country of origin for legal reasons. These may need to be projected, for the actual conversion of dividends implies a transaction risk beyond the translation of the underlying income. Forward hedges, of course, may cover both the income effect and the conversion risk.

Even if no dividend is declared, forecasting the income stream permits forward cover by the parent (when allowed) and protection of the group income statement. A deeper analysis, related to that for economic exposure in the balance sheet, may go beyond budget figures and attempt to break down the income of an exporting subsidiary as to currency. Again, ratio analysis can be used. This more sophisticated approach would analyse the sensitivity of gross income reported by the subsidiary to actual parity change, in conjunction also with its balance sheet commitments in those same currencies.

Absolute accuracy concerning future positions is not completely critical, since it is unobtainable in any case and firms cover their exposures in a general, rounded-up manner, normally with slight overcoverage to compensate for the inaccuracies of forecasting.

To perceive the direction over time, with the magnitude and timing at least roughly outlined, is the first and indispensable step in setting a strategy of optimal response to exposure. This in turn allows internal or external action to reduce the probable effect of parity changes before they occur.

Results of Proper Identification

From the combination of exposure identification reports, the group treasury should be able to depict:

(a) The present balance sheet position, by currency of the group and each affiliate.
(b) The future balance sheet position by currency similarly, if more crudely.
(c) A perception of the economic exposure, again by currency, faced by the subsidiaries.
(d) The future income or dividend streams and their currency breakdown.

The summary position of the group, from a translation viewpoint, can then be plotted by currency over several time periods. While not an exact measure, the table in Figure 3 would resemble the result of this summary. Actual and forecast positions by currency are given as the net position of exposed assets over exposed liabilities (long positions) or the reverse (short positions). The projected trends in balance sheet positions are immediately apparent. Income can be similarly projected. From the amalgamation of both summaries, the impact on the group can be analysed as the next step of the exchange management process.

Figure 3. Group exposure report. Net consolidated global position by currency.
Exposed assets over/(under) exposed liabilities
($ million equivalents)

	Actual Dec. 31, 1975	Forecast June 30, 1976	Forecast Dec. 31, 1976
Deutsche mark	$4.6	$3.8	$2.6
Dutch guilder	(3.3)	(3.3)	1.0
French franc	(4.9)	(2.3)	(3.5)
Belgian franc	1.8	1.0	2.4
Norwegian kroner	0.3	0.6	0.9
Pound sterling	(4.5)	3.3	4.7
Swiss franc	(1.3)	(1.4)	(1.4)
Italian lira	6.7	7.7	9.1
Danish kroner	2.8	2.8	2.8
Spanish peseta	10.5	14.0	9.8
Australian dollar	6.2	6.7	8.5
Canadian dollar	9.3	5.6	0.8
Japanese yen	2.3	4.7	6.8

CHAPTER 5

Identification of Exchange Exposure,
B: A Model Information System

This chapter shows a model information system consisting of a series of interlocking reports which encompass the elements described in Chapter 4. Each firm will wish to review its own reporting requirements on the basis of corporate structure, type of risk and cost of implementation. As already stated, an adequate reporting system is the foundation of exchange management. Although it appears a truism, risk positions cannot be managed without prompt identification of their magnitude and trends.

Good exposure management systems need also to be integrated into the overall financial management of the firm: its cash and liquidity concerns and the separate planning function rely on similar information. In the best systems, one consistent set of data can fulfil all the different management requirements and enhance the understanding of each area.

Following the logical sequence of the previous chapter, a model information system would consist of a series of interlocking elements, as follows.

Basic Translation Exposure Reports
1. Detailed Balance Sheets
The central control point would receive a detailed balance sheet monthly from each major subsidiary, containing its intercompany positions and with an exact breakdown by currency, shown in Figure 4.

For the smaller company, and in larger organizations when it takes longer to produce balance sheets, a flash report by telex along the lines of Figure 5 could be used.

2. Balance Sheet Forecasts
Depending on the complexity and sophistication of the group, the full balance sheet format can be used to forecast exposures in the future. Again, the currency breakdown is critical.

3. Exchange Exposure Reports
A subsititute or complement to the balance sheet approach is to have each subsidiary prepare a monthly exposure report, which does not

Figure 4. Balance sheet
(000)

	$	£	DM	FF	etc.
Subsidiary:					
Location:	Individual currencies				
Date:	listed by column				
Assets					
Cash and short-term investments					
Accounts receivable: Third party					
Intercompany					
Short-term loans to affiliated companies					
Inventory					
Pre-paid taxes and other expenses					
Total current assets					
Long-term investments and advances					
Net property, plants and equipment					
Other assets					
Total assets					
Liabilities					
Short-term debt					
Current portion of long-term debt					
Accounts payable: Third party					
Intercompany					
Accrued expenses					
Short-term intercompany debt					
Provision for taxes, other current					
Total current liabilities					
Other liabilities					
Long-term debt					
Long-term intercompany loans					
Total liabilities					
Net worth					
Common stock					
Other equity accounts					
Retained earnings					
Total net worth					
Total liabilities and net worth					

require a full accounting process. This provides not only the key elements of group exposure, but also helps to identify the economic exposure of subsidiaries. Such a report is shown in Figure 6, and is based on the FASB translation convention. Obviously, any other convention used by a company can be integrated into such a report. Hedges are also shown, as these bring back the foreign currency position, plus or minus, of the subsidiary to an equivalent amount in its own currency. As an example, a subsidiary in Belgium of a U.K. group

Figure 5. 'Flash' report by telex (to show quickly the main exposed positions by currency)

Cash/short-term investments	DM	100		
Accounts receivable	DM	80	SF	10
Intercompany receivables	$	10		
Overdrafts	—			
Accounts payable	DM	60	Hfl	5
Intercompany payables	$	20		
Hedges outstanding	Hfl	5	maturity 11/30/76	

(To that short cable could be added any other essential items, such as outstanding credit facilities unused, borrowing or investment interest rates, etc. Its advantage is that it can be submitted right after the end of each month, or even weekly, to give an immediate picture of the main exposures, both translation and economic.)

Figure 6. Exchange exposure report
(000)

Subsidiary:	
Location:	
Date:	

Local currency assets
  Cash
  Short-term investments
  Accounts receivable
  Pre-paid expenses
  Other current assets	

Total local currency assets	

Local currency liabilities
  Accounts payable
  Accrued expenses and other
  Short-term debt
  Long-term debt	

Total local currency liabilities	
Net local currency assets	

Foreign currency assets
  Item   Amount (in 000 foreign currency units)

Foreign currency liabilities
  Item   Amount (in 000 foreign currency units)

Forward contracts
  Currency bought/sold   Rate   Maturity

has dollar export receivables and Deutsche mark payables. Both may be covered forward in the Belgian forward markets and the subsidiary decides to do so. If it owes DM500,000 and will receive $100,000, both now hedged, the parent position in Belgian francs is increased by the Belgian franc equivalent of $100,000 and is decreased by the Belgian franc equivalent of DM500,000. The exact amounts of the Belgian franc changes can be determined from the actual forward rates of both contracts.

4. Reports on a Cash Flow Basis

An alternate approach is to base exposure on future cash flows. For instance, a Swedish multinational requires no specific balance sheets, but manages the operations of its dozen domestic subsidiaries by an array of cash flow reports. These include:

> yearly budget, updated quarterly;
> 13-month report of cash inflows and disbursements in foreign currency, updated each month;
> 4-week aggregate cash forecast, broken out by currency;
> daily call to the headquarters, notifying it of domestic funds needed or surplus to operations, and of exact foreign currency amounts to be received/paid 2 days hence.

This cash flow basis certainly identifies all transactional exposure and provides a rough basis for ascertaining the probable accounting risks.

5. Hedging Reports

Whether or not if a full balance sheet approach is adopted, separate information on all hedges by any affiliates must be received. This can be added on the bottom of the balance sheet report or cable or required as a separate form; it should include each individual hedge, rate and maturity. This is not only critical for the reason explained in section 3 above, but also in the U.S. for income reporting purposes, as forward contracts are now to be evaluated and their imputed gains or losses taken into group income at the closing date, unless they represent an exact hedge of outstanding commitments. As is shown in Chapter 8, subsidiaries should not be allowed to hedge their positions independently without the review of the parent finance department; such a report is a cross-check that they are complying with this policy. Total forward contracts and the results of market changes affecting their value can then be summarized at parent finance department level.

Economic Exposure Elements
6. Cash Forecasts

These will probably already exist in the company in the form of budget, sales or production forecasts but must be integrated with the above exposure reports if the balance sheet approach described above is accepted. Without a breakdown by currency, they are only of general use. Their value here is to identify liquidity positions of the subsidiaries and to indicate economic exposure elements. A typical cash reporting form, used by an international consumer products group, is shown in Figure 7.

Figure 7

Cash Report for Month Ending . . . .

Currency . . . .   Rate of exchange . . . .

Bank Balance
(indicate time deposits and currency where not local)
(000)

Bank	Rate earned	Amount

Securities
Intercompany balances
Customers drafts discounted
Bank loans + overdraft (list by bank)

Estimated Cash Positions for 3 Months
(000)

	Month 1		Month 2		Month 3	
	LC	FC	LC	FC	LC	FC*
Actual Receipts						
Accounts receivable						
Bank loans						
Intercompany loans						
Other						
Total receipts						
Disbursements						
Suppliers						
Bank loans						
Capital expenditures						
Taxes						
Salaries						
Other						
Total disbursements						
Balance						
Add: previous balance						
Balance, end of month						

---

*LC = Local Currency
FC = Foreign Currency

7. *Inventory Analysis*

Chapter 3 has already described the special position of inventory held abroad and the different types of risks it presents. If a company is in the position of having a split nature in its inventory, it may wish to break its report into locally exposed and non-locally exposed inventory. Some large chemical manufacturers do this by breaking that balance sheet item into two categories:

Inventory carried at local value
Inventory carried at international value.

In both cases, the rule of cost or market is still followed in establishing the underlying value. In a more advanced form, inventory analysis concerning future sales and sourcing patterns can be the subject of a separate report (Figure 8). This provides guidelines for the range of internal adjustments open to the very large international firms, but is not applicable to most companies.

Figure 8. Inventory analysis

	Local value	Relevant currencies		
I — A. Inventory sourced abroad in foreign currency, to be sold domestically				
B. Inventory sourced domestically and to be sold domestically				
C. Inventory sourced domestically and to be sold abroad				
D. Total inventory				

II — Comments on
    A. Elasticity of demand of inventory or major product groups
    B. Continuation of sourcing pattern

Ability to Adjust Intercompany Positions

A major tool open to the multinational company, if not to exporters and importers, is the ability to adjust intercompany positions. This involves the timing of payments, the currency of transactions and to some degree their price.

On existing outstanding intercompany items, the acceleration or deceleration of settlement will change the exposure of both companies.

The whole area of such 'leading/lagging' is controversial. Some observers see this as having a major detrimental effect on the monetary policy of central banks, others as a means of tax avoidance. As Chapter 7 will show, leading/lagging normally has strict parameters, in the form of a range of actual exchange control limits.

Where leading/lagging is permitted and used by a company, the finance department should require an intercompany transaction report showing which affiliates will pay to which others. This must include all payments where regulatory constraints insist on settlement, and others expected to be made under standard intercompany terms. Figure 9 gives an example.

Figure 9. Next period's intercompany settlements

Period from:		to:	
(000)			

Paying company: . . . .

Location: . . . .

Date: . . . .

	Amount	Currency
Due to affiliates in:		
U.K.		
Italy		
Germany		
France		
Canada		
Other		

This would cover a period of 2, 4 or more weeks depending on the size and complexity of intercompany transactions. It includes all items which must be made for regulatory reasons, and those other outstanding transactions expected to be settled.

Basic Constraints on Position Adustments

Information on the ability to change or cover exposed positions should be maintained in the form of a data bank at the Head Office. This would basically include the technical parameters within which the company and its affiliates operate and comprise the exchange control, monetary and fiscal restrictions imposed by each government. The following are the principal areas of limitation:

(i) export/import transactions:
   credit terms
   restrictions on leading/lagging

restrictions on currency of billing
required use of letter of credit, etc.;
 (ii) forward cover restrictions on:
final maturity
banks used
type of transactions where cover is permissible;
(iii) lending to companies abroad (intercompany or otherwise);
(iv) borrowing from companies abroad (intercompany or otherwise);
 (v) maintaining foreign currency accounts (domestically or abroad)
length of time funds can be so held
in-flow/out-flow matching requirements
interest factors;
(vi) withholding taxes on loans to/from abroad (intercompany or
otherwise);
(vii) double taxation treaties.

One reporting element encompasses regulatory constraints, liquidity implications and leading/lagging costs in a simple format, reproduced in Figure 10. The minimum and maximum days columns show the limits within which intercompany settlements can be delayed or accelerated without impinging upon exchange control limits. In the 'acceleration' section, the first two columns show whether a subsidiary has in fact the excess borrowing capacity or short-term investments it can liquidate to provide funds for a premature payment, which represents funds it did not expect to lose before maturity. The cost of such additional borrowings is given. When a subsidiary is allowed to lag its settlements, the interest saving of any debt reduction is shown. If it puts those funds in short-term deposits (when there is, in fact, a short-term money market), the potential yield is estimated. All of those factors can be up-dated weekly or monthly, depending on the nature of the firm and the extent of its use of this technique.

This is an excellent way to tie in several reporting threads in one standard montly report. It strongly stresses cost/yield aspects, rather than the more general 'seat-of-the-pants' feeling many companies appear to use. It is simple and inexpensive to instal, having the virtue of tying in liquidity considerations with actual market and regulatory parameters without proliferation of reports.

A company may wish to include additional data on local debt and credit market instruments, and the present rates on both sides of the market. It is not hard to visualize what type of information is required by the central treasury, but less easy to obtain it on an ongoing basis. Two possible solutions suggest themselves:

1. To make subsidiaries responsible for keeping the array of data elements current for their country of operation; or

Figure 10. Payment adjustment costs, yields and constraints

Subsidiary	If payments are accelerated from						If payments are delayed from				
	Minimum days	Total S.T. credit lines	Unused credit	Cost	Reduction of S.T. investment	Present yield	Maximum days	Pre-payable debt	Interest saving	S.T. investment availability	Interest yield
A											
B											
C											

2. To find an international bank source which will provide the range of necessary answers on a continuous basis and at short notice.

Rolling Report on Exchange Gains and Losses

A final type of report can be used throughout the year to evaluate the performance of the company in terms of its exchange gains and losses in foreign exchange. This management tool would also be prepared on a rolling basis; in one multinational this is done monthly and broken down into four headings:

1. Realized gains or losses on receivables and payables;
2. Realized inventory gains and losses;
3. Translation gains and losses;
4. Long-term debt effects.

The format used is reproduced in Figure 11.

Summary of Reporting Forms Needed

The treasurer will wish to have a combination of reports, at the suggested following frequencies:

Translation Data
Present balance sheet by currency, monthly
Present income statement, monthly
Exposure reports, including hedges, monthly.

Forecast Data
Future balance sheet projections, on a monthly or quarterly rolling basis.
Coming year's income projections, at least by quarter.

Liquidity Forecast (Rolling)
Cash budget by currency: 5 weeks forward; quarterly by month; annually by quarter.

Reports to Understand Economic Exposure
Inventory analysis, etc.

Structural Constraint Reports
Data bank on parameters updated as changes occur.
Leading/lagging report, monthly or more frequently.

Exchange Profit/Loss Analysis Report

Figure 11. Analysis of exchange profit and loss

(losses shown as debits)
(000)

Month ending......... 1975

Subsidiary	Month				Year to Date			
	Realized gains/losses accounts, receivable accounts payable	Realized gains/losses in inventory	Other adjustments	Long-term debt	Realized gains/losses accounts, receivable accounts payable	Realized gains/losses in inventory	Other adjustments	Long-term debt

This may appear to be a costly, even idealistic system. However, the best managed of the international firms already have a similar methodology and many medium-sized multinationals are rapidly building up such a system. At a second glance, it can be seen that all the internal data concerning present positions are already available in the various record-keeping locations of the company. Obtaining this type of information is often only a process of reorganization and redirection. Forecasting changes is difficult, but necessary, and the analytical effort going into that process may have educational spin-offs. Determining regulatory constraints is a fairly mechanical exercise. The costs of not having these types of information arise in foreign exchange losses which were not properly identified or anticipated, in the cost of covering amounts larger than necessary, or in foregone opportunity gains. Since these costs are substantially greater under floating rates, the effort to obtain and project company exposure positions systematically appears moderate. From that basis, an analysis of possible currency movements as they relate to those positions follows.

CHAPTER 6

Determination of Potential Impact on the Firm

After developing a structured reporting system with adequate forecasting elements, which takes into account the particular characteristics
of a firm, the corporate treasury should be in a position to review the
company's present and future exchange risks in each currency on a
continuous basis. The underlying data will permit this identification of
exposure at any level of the group, from the consolidated parent
balance sheet down to the smallest foreign subsidiary. At this point it is
possible to calculate the potential impact of any rate changes on the
company, based on its present and future positions and tax considerations.

Assessing Market Trends

Determining the impact of rate changes is a process of predicting
currency market trends and calculating their probable effect on the
specific positions of the firm. The assessment of market patterns was
difficult enough to achieve in Bretton Woods days; it now presents the
international corporation with even greater uncertainty.

Market-trend assessments can be obtained from three basic sources:
in-house economist departments, bank and professional economists and
traders. Predictions from all of these have certain limitations, depending
on the time period of risk involvement and the range of probability
needed for decision-making. As shown below, the first two sources are
primarily useful for longer-term predictions which go beyond the usual
time concern of the treasury.

1. For What Time Periods Should Trends be Assessed?

First, the treasurer should decide for which time periods market-
trend analysis is necessary for hedging decisions. This will rarely go out
beyond one year.

An immediate period for analysis should be a 3—6 month trading
horizon, which will cover most types of export and import transactions.
Imports and exports tend to have credit terms of up to 6 months (the
median limitation of the majority of exchange control systems); thus
the resulting payables and receivables, also any short-term borrowings
to finance or hedge those items, will fall into this horizon.

The second, complementary reference period is up to one year forward, focusing on the next balance sheet closing date, since this will determine the ultimate effect of rate changes on the next set of financial statements. The treasurer will be concerned with the potential impact of rate movements on present positions and those expected to arise before closing date, when various assets and liabilities will be translated at new rates, as shown in Chapter 2. He may also consider the probable result of consolidating income streams produced in foreign currencies over the financial period. This type of analysis requires an intermediate range rate forecast to deal with accounting/translation exposure more than with transaction risks.

Only long-term decisions — concerning direct investment, for instance — involve currency judgments much beyond those two horizons; it is difficult in any case to judge what importance the possible future exchange rate in a foreign country should have in the investment decision. The decision to instal, purchase or increase production facilities abroad should first be based on economic and political assessments, as well as calculations involving labour supply and relations, raw material availability, proximity to markets and regulatory environment.

On the other hand, the investment decision will normally imply long-term borrowing and this does indeed require long-term rate assessment. One cannot consider only the rate of interest in comparing the true cost of two long-term debt alternatives. The possibility of appreciation or depreciation of the currency borrowed relative to the base currency must be included in the analysis. Many U.S. firms which borrowed Deutsche marks in the 1960s found to their chagrin that the total dollar expense was much greater than had been anticipated.

Long-term currency movements are subject to much vicissitude and make the judgmental process very difficult. Yet some attempt to quantify the long-term rate movement effect on the direct investment decision financed by currency borrowing must be made. One possibility is discounted cash flow analysis, which calculates how much relative appreciation of the borrowed currency could be accepted in year 1, 2, ... x without increasing the total base currency cost (bringing into account the lower interest payment stream). From this assessment, the firm can formulate a borrowing policy based on that judgment, and its considered judgment as to the risk that the exchange rates in question will move beyond its point of indifference.

That task is part of the planning function and reiterates that the role of exchange exposure management, particularly its analytical elements, is interconnected with all management functions of the firm. Here, the treasury would be closely involved with planning decisions and would apply the same analytical techniques as for other exchange risk considerations.

Normally, though, in exchange risk management the treasurer will look at the two time horizons outlined above: 3—6 months for actual transactions and up to one year for translation risk. A confirmation of the relatively short-term horizons in exchange risk management is found in the market availability of forward contracts or other hedging devices. Forward purchases or sales are readily available in a number of currencies through 3 and 6 months up to one year. Thereafter the markets are considerably thinner; the amounts, currencies and maturities available are substantially reduced.

The treasurer must, therefore, obtain spot rate assessments for the short-term and the medium-term horizons described above. Unfortunately, the present market situation is such that predictions in the former area are cast in very broad bands of uncertainty, as shown in the next section.

2. Short-term Unpredictability

Changes in currency values arise from a number of factors. Obviously, the basic economic factors underlying a country's economy in general and its balance of payments in particular are primarily responsible for rate changes over time. Market participants, however, have a number of motives for buying and selling exchange which go beyond trade and capital reasons. Financial institutions may be involved in uncovered arbitrage; holders of liquidity move large volumes of currency across the exchanges because of short-term interest factors; at times, speculation plays a major role. The pronounced and rapid short-term movements of currencies in the mid-1970s appear to have no discernible or predictable pattern on which strategy could have been based, although some market participants feel that spot rates can be predicted correctly on average. While this may be sufficient for a trading entity which can reverse its position rapidly, it is not feasible

Figure 12. U.K. trade deficits and inflation rates

Monthly trade deficit (£000,000) 1975		Year to year consumer price index % increase
January	−287	19.9
February	−316	19.9
March	−119	21.2
April	−297	21.7
May	−48*	25.0
June	−180	26.1
Total	−1247	

*Affected by Port of London dock strike

for a corporation to undertake the same type of active trading and position adjustment. Economic theory has limited, if any, application in the short-term horizon.

An example of this may be instructive. The trade balance of the U.K. and its horrendous domestic inflation rate showed the patterns of Figure 12 in early 1975, continuing a marked degeneration during 1974.

At the same time, the rates of inflation of its main trading rivals/partners were sharply below the U.K. level. Representative examples are shown in Figure 13.

Figure 13. Trade figures and inflation rates for selected U.K. trading partners: first half 1975

	Balance of trade ($000)	Consumer price level (% in consumer prices June 30th, 1974 to June 30th, 1975)
France	1618	11.7
Germany	7636	6.4
Holland	12	10.3
U.S.	5443	9.3
Japan	1948	13.4

Source: O.E.C.D.

With all economic indications pointing to an unavoidable depreciation of the pound, its trade-weighted average volume hardly changed at all in the first 5 months of the year, as shown in Figure 14. This is generally believed to be due to the Arab-held funds in sterling, rather than Bank of England support or an identifiable lag in rate response to economic conditions. Originally attracted to London by the size of the market and high sterling interest rates, these funds became to a certain extent 'locked-in'; to take them out en masse would have meant a very large

Figure 14. Trade-weighted pound devaluation since February, 1971

	Month-end figures
December 31, 1974	−25.21
January 31, 1975	−25.89
February 28	−25.78
March 31	−25.60
April 30	−26.35

Source: World Financial Markets

drop in the sterling rate, thus immediately depreciating all sterling holdings (although the first to do so would have suffered little loss). Under this apprehension, such investments tended to be left in the U.K. markets.

(Of course, reality finally caught up with the pound's value after mid-summer 1975, when the trade-weighted devaluation fell sharply. The real point here is that basing short-term rate assessment and thus strategy in that period on economic factors would have led the treasurer to misleading conclusions.)

The Italian lira in 1974/early 1975 showed similar unpredictability. In that period, there was essentially no central government; massive strikes and labour unrest abounded. Capital flight abetted an already dismal balance of payments, and the oil crisis appeared to eliminate any chance of a lira recovery. The lira, however, appreciated slightly against the dollar and held its trade-weighted value in a manner which few observers could, or did, predict. Many other examples will be known to the reader.

Capital movements on the part of all financial market participants have become so large and volatile, often seeking a presumed safety (of the currency and the institution holding funds) that prediction of short-term spot rate movements is currently of little value. This presents the treasurer with great problems in determining the impact of unpredictable rates on presently exposed positions and those antici- pated in the near future.

Yet he must come to a policy of covering those transactions or leaving them open. This is still a process of determining the likely movement of short-term rates and the cost incurred in the firm's foreign currency positions if the *worst* possible outcome occurs. This probable cost can be compared with the known costs of hedging to establish a currency by currency strategy. Chapter 9 goes into this in detail.

3. Medium-range Movements

Medium-range movements of interest to the treasury were defined as falling in the 6—12 month range, concentrating on a horizon of one year forward. In this area, economic forces and principles have more validity and traditional economic indicators may be useful. Many sources provide an analytical framework to look at the longer-term economic outlook in major countries. These will depend on movements of

> the trade balance,
> invisibles account,
> short-term capital,
> long-term capital movements.

They will be correlated with trends of productivity, inflation rates and other factors affecting the international competitive stance of each country, such as the marginal propensity of a country to import, and of the rest of the world to buy its products. Estimates of balance of payments positions over time, following that type of analysis, have continued to be accurate within an acceptable range.

This approach is also encapsulated in the theory of Purchasing Power Parity (PPP) used to predict exchange rate movements. There is considerable academic work going on in this area, some of which appears to indicate that there is indeed a correlation between underlying economic factors and future spot exchange rates.[1] A second body of opinion, however, still holds that daily spot rate movement at any given period is more likely to be influenced by other factors, particularly short-term monetary flows. Furthermore, rate trends which ultimately may be more identifiable through analysis such as Purchasing Power Parity, are longer term in nature and involve a one to three year time span, which is less useful for the corporate treasurer.

There is a haziness in the intermediate term area of 6 months to 1 year out, the second principal time horizon. The degree of confidence in the ability to forecast falls here between the unpredictable short run and the more quantifiable longer term economic trends. Many corporate decisions must be made in that middle ground where neither traders nor economist sources are of great help. This unpredictability, combined with adversion to risk, has probably resulted in increased hedging by corporations since the advent of floating rates.

However, by analysis of the general performance and usefulness of the various forecasting sources listed in the next section, the treasurer can eventually formulate his own decision as to the high and low parameters of the expected movement of any currency. Some treasurers find it instructive to chart the rate prediction record of their bank and consulting firm sources against actual market developments.

4. Sources of Economic Analysis/Rate Predictions

In-house economists in larger companies provide continual analyses of economic conditions in countries where the subsidiaries operate or the firm is contemplating investment. In some cases, they furnish rate projections as well and are consulted constantly on investment/hedging/borrowing decisions.

Statistical data themselves are available from each government and central bank, as well as from international organizations such as the EEC, OECD or the UN Commissions. Problems might arise for the company user in the lack of timeliness of data, language of publication and basis of computation. The quality, even authenticity, of data in many countries can be unsatisfactory.

As an alternative, a number of sources — primarily economic consult-

54

ants and commercial banks — offer economic studies and statistical analyses to their customers. These can supplement or replace in-house analytic capability and provide important guidelines to economic developments abroad, developments which also affect corporate areas other than exchange management. Such studies synthesize a large body of statistical information and personal contacts and often furnish an efficient array of information at low cost compared to that involved in setting up a full in-house analytical capability.

For short-run market movements, bank traders provide descriptions of supply, demand, interest rate and other factors affecting spot rate movements and forward market trends. Being intimately involved in the markets, they can readily see all participants, including those bidding speculatively. In general, though, they are busiest and hardest to reach just when their advice is most sought, and rarely offer precise spot rate predictions in any case.

Depicting Possible Rate Changes

Whatever sources and analyses are used, the range of future rate changes in various time periods must be assimilated by the treasury for comparison with its own projected positions. Rates can be forecast as a single point, or as a range of all possibilites with or without probabilities attached to specific rates. Thus, the future pound/dollar spot rate for a date 3 months ahead could be predicted as $2.00, or within a range of $1.97—2.05. The full range including all reasonably possible outcomes can also usefully be put into histogram form, as in Figure 15.

Figure 15. Histogram of £/$ spot rate possibilities at 3 months hence

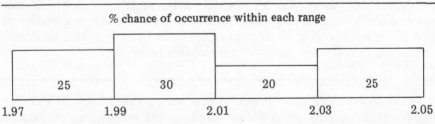

% chance of occurrence within each range

| 25 | 30 | 20 | 25 |

1.97   1.99   2.01   2.03   2.05

The analysis of histogram predictions is more useful for the treasurer, since the one point prediction with X% chance does not tell the ranges of possible change clearly enough. The histogram could well be bimodal, as Figure 16 shows in an extreme case.

Here, there is a high probability of a future pound/dollar spot rate of around $2.00 and a smaller chance of major pound depreciation (such a histogram could reflect the expected continuance or omission of official support or speculation). Basing a corporate covering strategy only on the $2.00 rate could be totally wrong.

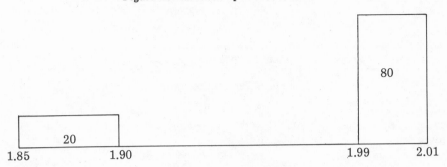

Figure 16. Bimodal spot rate estimate

Applying Rate Forecasts to the Company's Position

The next step is a composite analysis of future rate changes with present company positions and future positions where materially different. This might take the form of Figure 17.

Figure 17. Effects of revaluation/devaluation on ABC company's present exposure

Currency	Expected rate range at (closing) date	% Maximum expected change	Maximum gross translation gain (loss) ($000)	Gain (loss) to income
Canada	0.98—0.99	+1—(1)	(46)	(4)
U.K.	2.00—2.05	0—(2)	126	5
France	4.30—4.40	+2—(3)	(5)	—
Italy	680—730	0—(10)	(47)	(10)
Germany	2.50—2.55	+2—+4	89	12
Holland	2.60—2.65	+1—+3	2	—

Such a summary consolidates the range of rate predictions, the translation losses at parent level and the income effect, which should be calculated on an after-tax basis. Some companies prefer to prepare such calculations in actual amounts, based on the worst possible outcome (if a point estimate is used, the calculation is similar). Others compute translation or income effects by calculating the gain or loss on a per share basis.

The calculation in Figure 17 is used for hedging future consolidation and income effects. Thereafter, the character of the company's response will be determined by its own policies, risk profile and cost of hedging.

The same analysis can be applied to the short-term economic exposure of subsidiaries. A French subsidiary of a U.S. company may have the following balance sheet (currency commitments shown in brackets):

Example E
Short-term economic exposure of French subsidiary

French franc equivalents

Cash	100 (FF)	Short-term debt	400 (FF)
Accounts receivable	2000 (FF)	Accounts payable	600 (DM)
Inventory	1500 (FF)		1000 (FF)
		Intercompany debt	1000 ($)
		Taxes payable	200 (FF)
Total Current Assets	3600	Total Current Liabilities	3200
Intercompany receivables	400 ($)	Long-term debt	1000 (FF)
			1000 ($)
Plant and equipment	3000 (FF)	Equity	1800 (FF)
Total Assets	7000	Total Liabilities + Equity	7000

The range of cross-rate predictions for the French franc, U.S. dollar and Deutsche mark will make the operational risks for the French subsidiary immediately apparent. In translation terms, intercompany items and the dollar debt will not be considered exposed. The French subsidiary's own transaction exposures, however, are as follows (French franc equivalents):

	Plus	Minus	Net
Dollars (short-term)	400	(1000)	(600)
(long-term)	—	(1000)	(1000)
Deutsche marks		(600)	(600)

It is significantly exposed in dollars and Deutsche marks if the franc should weaken. To assess the French subsidiary's transaction exposure, the treasurer would calculate the effect of intercompany debt in the whole structure of intercompany accounts, the timing and repayment schedule of third party long-term debt, the same for Deutsche mark creditors and the tax effect of any rate changes. This is carried out in addition to the assessment of the parent company's own French franc exposure.

Tax Effects

The comparison of company positions and rate trends has little meaning unless the resultant fiscal effects are ascertained. There the dichotomy between taxable and non-taxable gains and losses is apparent. Balance sheet gains (or losses) on translation rarely have a taxable effect.[1] Losses on conversion usually have a direct fiscal effect on the parent or at subsidiary level.

Intercompany loans provide a typical example. A German subsidiary may, without restriction on the German side, make a Deutsche mark to a French affiliate. Before the loan matures, the Deutsche mark appreciates sharply against the franc and the French subsidiary incurs a realized exchange loss on repayment. The loss is deductible against French income taxes, but the German subsidiary shows neither gain nor loss. On consolidation, no pre-tax effect in either direction will be shown, since the dollar value of the German receivable will be off-set by a decrease in the French payable. The net tax effect is favourable, however, since the French tax burden is lower after deductions for realized exchange losses.

Any calculation of impact, therefore, must look once again 'beyond the balance sheet' to determine the after tax effect of any rate movement and any hedging tactic. Chapter 13 goes into this in some detail.

Notes
1. See Gailliot, Henry J., 'Purchasing power parity as an explanation of long-term changes in exchange rates'. *Journal of Money, Credit and Banking*, August 1970.
2. An exception is Brazil, which currently allows tax deductions for unrealized book losses on certain foreign currency loans.

CHAPTER 7

Hedging Methods: Internal

The international company has a variety of techniques at its disposal to neutralize, minimize or avoid exchange risks. These methods are loosely lumped together as 'covering' or 'hedging'. In this volume, *covering* is defined as the purchase or sale of foreign exchange forward to offset completely the risk of fluctuation in a rate of exchange when payments are to be made or received in that foreign currency in the future, or balance sheet positions to be translated at a closing spot rate. *Hedging*, a broader term, is defined as all actions taken to change the exposed positions of a company in a currency or currencies.

The application and selection of such techniques vary directly and proportionately with the complexity and international penetration of the firm. Thus the exporting/importing company has only certain hedging methods available, while a much fuller range is open to the true multinationals.

Exchange risk management in both types of companies has two basic considerations: the appropriateness of internal as well as external hedging possibilities and the impact and limitations of regulations, tax effects and cost factors, which must be ascertained in advance. All techniques used to change or reduce risk have a basic cost (which can be positive), although this may fall in marketing areas, rather than be directly explicit. All are also affected by the accounting convention used to translate foreign currency items, which shapes the way in which the corporation will select and apply hedging techniques.

Before the better-known *external* techniques are analysed, each type of company should consider which *internal* hedging methods are open to it and at what cost, which is the subject of this chapter. These basically fall into asset and liability adjustments; they are further divided into types of actions which can be taken in regard to existing transactions or positions, and those which can be made before the company is committed to a pattern of risks. Certain more sweeping structural changes which help to centralize or redirect risks of the group are reviewed.

Internal Techniques Affecting Outstanding Positions

1. Pre-payment of Existing Third Pary Commitments

Exchange risks arising from third party transactions fall into export, import or financial categories. Outstanding third party export receivables are fixed as to currency and maturity and cannot be changed by internal adjustments. Import commitments, however, normally can be pre-paid if the currency in which they are invoiced is expected to appreciate vis-à-vis that of the importer. Likewise, hard currency loans, where there is a pre-payment option, may be paid down. The immediate cost of such transactions is the domestic financing expense (or the interest foregone) from the time of early payment to the original maturity. The principal restrictions are in the exchange control regulations of the importer's country (which may rule out pre-payments) or of the exporting/lending country, which may prohibit the premature receipt of funds by explicit decree or financial charges.

2. Intercompany Term Adjustment

Greater scope is offered in intercompany positions, where, again, within regulatory limits, the original payment dates can be accelerated or delayed to change the basic position of the group in a specific currency. Commonly called leading and lagging, this is a widely used and legitimate technique to combat risk or to shift liquidity.

Some of the basic criteria behind leading and lagging have already been discussed in Chapter 5. A major factor is that funds are taken from one affiliate more rapidly than expected and given to the other before anticipated; both impacts should be known. The cost/yield aspects of the liquidity being transferred are thus critical in the adjustment decision, since the costs of augmenting one subsidiary's liquidity could outweigh the expected exchange gains.

Perhaps a comment on the larger implications of leading/lagging is in order. By that mechanism, funds are transferred from one country to another without a direct timing relationship to their trade patterns. Many commentators have pointed out the possible resultant impact on the domestic liquidity or exchange rates of certain countries with high foreign trade ratios. So far, these effects have primarily remained potential, rather than actual.

The corporate effect of leading and lagging is felt through intercompany positions, which are altered in advance of movements of exchange rates. Example F shows the position of Danish and German affiliates of a multinational company with and without pre-paying an intercompany account.

The use of intercompany account adjustment is widespread, since it is both a means to move liquidity and to change exposure risk. Furthermore, this technique is more appropriate in many cases than straightforward intercompany loans. In recent years, the U.S. Internal

Example F
Leading/Lagging between two subsidiaries

ABC Denmark owes DM200,000 to ABC Germany for a trade import. Normal repayment terms are 90 days and cross-rates start at DKr2 = DM1 = \$0.40.

The balance sheet items in question are as follows:

ABC Denmark		ABC Germany		ABC Group	
	(DKr)		(DM)		(\$)
Cash	100	Accounts receivable	200	Cash	20
Inventory	400	Equity	200	Inventory	80
Accounts payable	400			Equity	100
Equity	100				

If the Danish kroner depreciates 10% before maturity, there is a net pre-tax loss to the Danish subsidiary, and to the group:

Cash	100	Accounts receivable	200	Cash	18.2
Inventory	400	Equity	200	Inventory	72.7
Accounts payable	440			Equity	90.9
Equity	60				

If the payment from Denmark to Germany is accelerated and completed before devaluation, the cash is transferred to Germany and the result of the parity change is lessened:

Cash	100	Cash	200	Cash	98.2
Equity	100	Equity	200	Equity	98.2

Combined with other hedging techniques, the group would show little effect from the Danish kroner devaluation.

Revenue Service has generally allowed intercompany accounts to be extended to at least 6 months without imputing interest, while interest must be charged at reasonable rates on intercompany loans.

Leading/lagging appears controllable if central banks construct efficient parameters on leading/lagging, such as those imposed by the German *Bardepotgesetz*. In that so far unique case, the German authorities established the trade terms which were customary ('handelsüblich') for each major industry group. Firms were allowed to grant or accept credit terms only within the framework of their industry. They could not lag payments out of, or accept earlier than normal payments into, Germany, without incurring an obligation to put a fixed percentage of the additional funds (typically 50%) into interest-free reserves at the Bundesbank. This effectively curbed leading/lagging and brought its unwanted effects of increasing German liquidity to a minimum. Borrowing from abroad was similarly restricted. The mechanism proved effective in practice, although warranting an army of clerks. It could probably be used just as effectively in reverse to keep funds within a country and is much less inhibiting to world trade than either import quotas or deposits (granted that the two latter techniques are targeted at a different area of balance of payments flows).

3. Exposure Netting

Exposure netting is not so much a technique as an acceptance of open positions in two (or more) currencies, which are considered to balance each other and, therefore, to require no further internal or external hedging.

Even in floating rate periods, there are a number of currencies which have tended to move in close conjunction. The best known example of this is the European 'snake' — the Deutsche mark, Dutch guilder, Belgian franc and other currencies of countries which have agreed to keep their spot rates within a narrow range. Other arrangements exist from time to time, such as the unilateral decision of Austria to support the schilling within a close parameter of the German mark.

The relevance of this is that a short position in such a currency can be considered offset to some degree by a long position in a closely related currency. Thus an exporter with Belgian franc payables and Dutch guilder receivables might decide that these two positions covered each other and that forward contracts were not necessary. Carrying the analogy further, a firm might decide that a long position in a traditionally hard currency, Deutsche mark or yen, would balance eventual depreciation of holdings in a softer currency.

It should be stressed that this tactic is fundamentally more risky, as it entails a degree of speculation. (True speculation is accepting positions in currencies in which the firm has no natural inflows or outflows, such as U.S. railroad companies borrowing Swiss francs in the late 1960s.) The historical patterns of or stated agreements concerning currency movements do not always bear true. The pattern can change or the timing vary from roughly coterminous to a wide lag. Worse yet, the company's analysis of currency covariances can be faulty. In one disastrous case, a major multinational in the 1960s, worried about its Deutsche mark short position, decided to cover by exposure netting. It thereupon borrowed an equal amount of Dutch guilders which were switched into the parent currency. When both currencies strongly appreciated against that currency, its losses were doubled rather than reduced. On the other hand, certain bilateral groupings of currencies — again the Deutsche mark and the Austrian schilling — have been predictable enough at times to allow a limited amount of exposure netting. Even here, the correct approach should be to weigh the apparent movement of each currency against methods by which a corporation can protect itself against, or benefit from, that movement, to come up with the selection of the correct method. Exposure netting may involve an opportunity cost in not adopting a more profitable or less costly method and, therefore, cannot be generally recommended.

Internal Techniques Affecting Future Positions

The above techniques — chiefly lagging or leading payments — form a limited and short term range of hedging techniques related to existing positions only. Anticipatory exposure management strategy for the longer term offers a greater variety of useful risk adjustment possibilities. These fall into two types: changes in pricing/currency billing policy and changes in balance sheet positions. Each is reviewed here.

1. Price Adjustments

All price increases which are aimed at reducing exposure losses are predominantly affected by marketing considerations, which must be decided by the individual firm in its unique context. Assuming, however, that these place no insuperable barrier to price increases, the latter offer the possibility to increase the volume of receipts in a 'soft' or suspect currency.

a. Local subsidiary price increases: Often the only way to protect against the negative effect of depreciation or devaluation of a local currency is for a local sales or manufacturing subsidiary to raise its prices before that occurs. This is particularly prevalent in South America, where there may be no forward market, local borrowing costs are astronomical and leading/lagging is not appropriate. If the local sales price can be raised before devaluation, the reported income stream and ultimate dividends are protected. This can be doubly important when, as is often the case, a local price freeze follows currency devaluation. (This of course raises the issue of whether prices should not be increased in any case, if market strength or customer demand permits. Probably so, but that is a sales/marketing department decision. The treasury input could be an important factor in pushing other departments into such a decision which has more than one justification.)

b. Export price increases: Export price increases depend even more on marketing factors, since there are often both international and local competitive products. When exports are denominated in a currency likely to depreciate, selective price increases can protect revenues just as local price adjustments do. A discount option for more prompt payment has somewhat the same effect.

c. Currency of billing changes: A more subtle price adjustment strategy is through the currency of billing. Many exporting companies appear absolutely hide-bound in this area. The author has dealt with dozens of companies, particularly in the U.S. and the U.K., which have traditionally billed in dollars or sterling respectively. Even after sharp and continual devaluation of either currency, little thought is given to billing in other currencies where possible.

Reasons for such an obdurate policy are usually:

'we always did it that way';
'our accounting systems won't permit other currency booking';
'our computer invoicing system can't be adjusted to raise invoices in other currencies than our own';
'it would confuse our customers/sales force';
'it would be speculative'.

All but the last excuse are very weak. A number of export markets would appear to have been lost in the 1960s by U.S. companies' unwillingness to bill in other than U.S. dollars. The converse effect is seen in the case of exporters in weak currency countries. If they switch to invoicing in currencies likely to appreciate against their own, opportunity gains could be achieved. This does, of course, require taking a view of and position in currencies not previously used for billing.

In the case of sterling, the opportunity costs of retaining pound invoices when the pound is under constant pressure are apparent. Many U.K. firms have strong market positions in their industry or in selected market areas such as the Commonwealth. There is no technical requirement to invoice only in pounds. A priori, it would appear that the individual elasticity of demand is such that the sales volume of many companies would not be affected by a switch from sterling (or any other home currency in similar cases) to that of the importer, or eventually a third currency.

Assuming that such a switch is made at roughly the current cross-rates of the two currencies, there is no immediate price increase. For example, if ABC Ltd.'s product sells for £100, and is now invoiced at Hfl545 (representing the equivalent parities at the time of change), there is no apparent difference to the Dutch importer, who owes Hfl545 in either case. Only if a later depreciation of the pound vis-à-vis guilders ensues, will the importer bear an opportunity cost in the form of foregone exchange profits from reduced payables.

Given the increased awareness of foreign exchange rates and movements, many foreign customers will be knowledgeable about the potential impact of such currency billing changes on their own company. Those having been in the position of owing dollars or sterling in the period since 1971 will have seen positive gains from time to time without any action on their part and may resist being billed in their own or other hard currency. This brings the analysis back to one of marketing strength, as well as the contemporary outlook for each currency.

The point here is that most exporters only look at the possibility of changing export currencies after a sharp fall in their own currency. That alternative should be a normal and regular part of hedging strategy setting and an accepted technique where appropriate. Its converse — billing in weaker currencies where the home currency is inherently strong — should likewise be considered if sufficient sales increases are fostered, with sufficient margins to allow external protection methods (forward markets, financing via the same currency, etc.).

Obviously, a measure of risk enters whether one switches from a supposedly weak currency of billing to a stronger one. No currency trends are so predictable, or so long-lived, that one can assume with certainty that a billing switch will remain as attractive in the future. Currencies of billing cannot always easily be reversed and clearly cannot be changed often. Once again, a variety of factors will influence this decision, which will have to be reviewed from time to time.

A more aggressive version of the same technique is to convert the selling price, not at the spot cross-rate, but at the forward rate for the maturity of the credit period offered. An English exporter in a seller's market might contemplate changing to Deutsche mark billing when the spot rate is £1 = DM5.30 and the 3 months rate DM5.23. Its new invoices could be calculated at the 5.23 rate, adding an automatic 5% to annual sales revenue even if no relative appreciation of the Deutsche marks takes place. If gauged correctly, the export has a price increase and an inherent hedge against its own currency.

No matter which rate is used, the exporter in a weak currency is also given the probability of increased profits in that it can sell the new hard currency receipts forward at a premium in normal markets. In essence, this transfers the profits made by export customers in buying its currency forward at a discount or paying less amounts of local currency for later import settlement, to the exporter.

d. Transfer pricing through the exchange rate. The most aggressive manifestation of the same function is to use the export currency of billing literally to transfer profits from one affiliate to another, i.e. to raise or lower intergroup selling prices by billing rate adjustments so that profits arise in hard currency or low-tax companies. This has been a well-known technique for tax strategy, sometimes with the misguided goal of tax minimization (rather than after-tax profit maximization, not necessarily the same). It could conceivably be used solely as a technique to shift exchange gains and losses.

However, the increasing constraints put on traditional transfer pricing sharply curtail that alternative advantage as well. The tax and customs officials who inspect intercompany pricing structures are knowledgeable and astute. A number of court cases have recently indicated their growing awareness of, and readiness to prosecute, transfer pricing arrangements. Given the wide variety of other legal hedging techniques, transfer pricing as an aggressive foreign exchange management device cannot be recommended. Intercompany billing rates should be kept within a reasonable range of spot rates, i.e. about 1% on either side of the market rate at invoice date.

2. Asset/Liability Management

The second major area of internal anticipatory changes in exposure management comes in asset or liability adjustment. This is related to leading/lagging in having the same goal: reduced assets/increased liabilities in currencies likely to depreciate, increased assets/reduced liabilities in hard currencies.

While a number of constraints on the manipulation of balance sheet positions exist, the logic is straightforward. For revaluation-prone situations, the techniques to consider are as follows.

a. Increase of net short term assets: Either the parent itself, or more likely, the subsidiary concerned will try to build up cash, short-term investments, receivables and/or inventories denominated in currencies expected to revalue. If the Deutsche mark were such a currency, a German subsidiary could be instructed to pay its bills as slowly as possible under constraints of supplier relationships, to convert other currency holdings or investments into Deutsche mark and to delay inter-company settlements or dividends. It might also delay its purchase of, or settlement for, raw materials. All these will build up its net short-term Deutsche mark asset position, which contains those items both always translated/consolidated at spot rates and likely to be realized in the near future.

b. Reduction of liabilities: The net increase of short-term asset positions could be achieved as well by reduction of group members' short-term debt denominated in hard currencies, pre-payment of hard currency payables and analogous techniques.

When a devaluation-prone currency is involved, the same techniques apply in reverse. Cash and short-term security holdings will be run down, local debt increased, certain payables accelerated, intercompany payments rescheduled. The goal will be to reduce long positions or to increase debt and other commitments in a currency to benefit from or be protected against its expected depreciation.

c. Long-term asset/liability changes: Longer-term balance sheet positions do not lend themselves easily to rapid reduction, although pre-payment of long-term debt is one possibility. Assets such as physical plant and equipment are, in any case, only considered exposed under the closing rate method. Occasionally techniques such as leasing can remove fixed assets from the direct balance sheet, although to little purpose unless held in a country whose currency is depreciating and accounted for under the closing rate convention.

Limitations on the range of these techniques, used in either direction, will be the actual regulatory limits of exchange control, the market structure, the attitude of lenders and creditors and any related tax implications.

Long-term Structural Changes

More sweeping than either price changes or balance sheet positioning are long-range structural changes to redirect and centralize exchange risks. The two most common methods are the export financing/factoring subsidiary and the full-scale intermediary company used to reinvoice group exports or imports. These are growing in importance, if at a slow rate, as the number of firms to which they may apply is limited.

1. Export Financing Vehicles

Hedging of foreign commitments, by whatever means, is constrained by the restrictions imposed by each exchange control and by exchange market structure. The typical situation is that each local affiliate must cover its own transaction exposures locally under specific external regulations. (Chapter 8 goes into this in more detail.) Market limitations, local restrictions and abilities may make that an inefficient process.

An imaginative way to rationalize this situation is to create a finance company vehicle which buys the export receivables of the group and assumes the credit risk and covering responsibility. This can be done through several types of vehicle companies (there are even a few full-fledged captive banks); the confirming house is representative.

A fully-owned vehicle is created, in the U.K. or elsewhere, which purchases the export receivables of each group member as created or buys outstanding receivables under previous agreement. The vehicle needs the freedom or specific exchange control permission to finance its receivable portfolio in the Euro-markets with the same or different currencies and with unmatched maturities. If such flexibility can be obtained, the export exchange risks of the group are centralized in this vehicle during the life of the receivables. Local affiliates sell their export receivables to it at full value (or discount them, depending on local requirements) and are out of the transaction. Normally, this will be done without recourse to the original seller.

The confirming house then can be used as a flexible finance vehicle. Its assets will consist of export receivables with varying dates and currencies, its liabilities of short-term borrowings. It can cover those risks and maturities exactly, or can leave them uncovered as to timing and amount as part of an overall risk strategy. Centralization in a vehicle operating essentially 'off-shore' in the Euro-markets gives a great deal more flexibility and the ability to put a trained group in charge of all such risks. Such a vehicle can usually be established with moderate capital input and legal costs (the former since its borrowings will presumably be guaranteed by the parent); it is, of course, fully taxable in the country of incorporation.

Other advantages of the confirming house concept also support financial management in a broader sense.

1. The vehicle gives an opportunity to offer third party customers abroad invoicing in their own currency. Since it should be appreciably easier for the vehicle company to match or cover foreign exchange exposure than the exporting companies, there would be more flexibility in offering any foreign customer the option of being invoiced in its own currency, rather than the exporter's.
2. By concentrating a portion of, if not all, intercompany receivables in the books of the finance house, offsetting possibilities may occur with the resultant conversion cost savings.
3. Export credit guarantees from government sources, such as the Export Credit Guarantee Department in the U.K. (ECGD) or the U.S. Federal Credit Insurance Agency (FCIA) are not affected.
4. Credit management can still be centred in the hands of the local exporting company, or the vehicle company can play an active part in the credit evaluation, terms and conditions.

2. Reinvoicing Vehicles

A finance/confirming house, however, can only react in the receivable portion of risks. Since it holds title solely to the underlying paper involved, legal recourse in the case of customer default is also more problematic. A more complex approach, involving greater expense and structural change, is to create a reinvoicing intermediary company. Such a vehicle takes actual title to the goods moving through a multinational group and can act as a central purchasing agent as well.

Such intermediary companies are usually located in a country with nominal exchange control and low rates of taxation, such as Switzerland or Bermuda. They are incorporated resident companies with a local board and full set of books. Their major role is typically to buy the exported products of the group, and to reinvoice these for sale on to the ultimate customers. The credit terms, currency of invoicing and price to the third party buyer are unchanged.

The reinvoicing takes place either manually or by computer and the actual goods are shipped as before, thus the tariff/customs framework is unaffected. This is particularly important in multinational groupings with advantageous internal tariff regulations, such as the EEC or EFTA.

The point of this procedure is to create intercompany payables/receivables that did not exist before, thereby redoubling the amount of flexibility offered in hedging external risks. For example, a group may have $50 million of intercompany sales, $50 million of third party exports and $25 million of third party imports, all in various currencies. The internal area of payment/currency adjustment lies in the credit period while intercompany payables are outstanding. If 90 days credit terms are company practice, then around $12.5 million of outstanding intercompany accounts would exist. Adding both exports and imports to the intercompany structure by reinvoicing creates an annual volume of $125 million; here 90 days average outstandings would result in some $31 million equivalent of intercompany payables at any given time.

The intermediary company may also buy from each exporting affiliate in its local currency, and purchase for them their imports, reinvoicing back in local currency. If carried out rigorously, this puts all the trading exposure of the group into a central entity.

The potential advantages of such centralization are listed below.

1. Local personnel, who may not be trained to deal with exposure risk and cannot know all company positions in any case, are left to concentrate on production, marketing or local financing.
2. Being centralized in one company, the identification of exposure and any requisite hedging are facilitated.
3. Some exposures may be mutually offsetting. For example, a U.K. subsidiary might owe dollars, a German subsidiary have dollar receivables. Ordinarily, both would cover these positions by forward contracts. If reinvoiced, the intermediary's dollar receivables and dollar payables might be internally offset, obviating the need for external hedges and reducing costs.
4. Centralized purchasing can bring organizational and/or cost savings. Third party import commitments can be reinvoiced to add to the portfolio of intercompany paper.
5. By creating a framework of intercompany transactions, where only third party flows had dominated before, a 'linkage' is created between affiliates. By leading or lagging of the underlying payments, liquidity can also be shifted, within limits, between countries.

There are several dozen such companies in existence, belonging to a variety of parents in different countries. Most were set up for tax purposes originally, although this has sharply been curtailed by 'Sub-part F' rules for U.S.-owned vehicles (see page 74). A few have been set up purely for International Money Management centralization purposes.

The intermediary company is no panacea and requires a considerable volume of trade to cover the costs of establishing and running it. As a negative aspect, it may bring closer scrutiny by tax, customs or central bank authorities and requires in any case considerable sophistication and expertise to run the complex book of receivables/payables created. The accounting side is not routine. The feasibility of such a company should be well established in advance from a cost/flexibility analysis.

Intermediary companies may have quite different, if complementary, justifications: financing or holding functions. In the more narrow area of foreign exchange risk management, their chief advantages are to create and expand the necessary centralization while offering more flexibility in dealing with perceived risk.

Summary of Internal Techniques and Limitations

Concurrently with the analysis of external ways to reduce exposure, the finance manager of an international company should examine the wide range of internal adjustment techniques open to it as a result of its structure. Where a single large exporter or importer is concerned, only limited methods, basically pre-payments and changing the currency of export invoicing, are available. In a multinational context, many more possibilities exist: leading or lagging of payments, changing of invoicing currencies, local price increases, exposure netting, can be considered. All fall under the cost/risk analysis necessary for all types of hedging; all should best be considered as available tools. In isolated cases, even new company vehicles can be applicable over the long range.

CHAPTER 8

Hedging Methods: External

The second area of hedging involves a concatenation of techniques available in external markets, applying to all types of companies with international involvement. They are also more clearly delineated and their cost usually can be precisely determined in advance. These fall into the following categories:

Forward exchange contracts;
Foreign currency loans;
Discount/sale of foreign receivables;
Retained currency accounts;
Borrowing/deposit arrangements in two currencies;
Factoring;
Leasing;
Export risk guarantees.

All but the last tend to involve existing or outstanding transactions; indeed, local exchange controls of most countries will not permit forward contracts or other similar currency operations by residents without appropriate visible underlying transactions, which must be checked by a commercial bank. Many of the institutional arrangements for such techniques can be negotiated in advance, in anticipation of future, as yet unbooked commitments. The appropriate forward exchange, discount or borrowing lines or accounts can be arranged so that new deals are immediately and often automatically brought into a hedged position. Rates used for illustration purposes are those prevailing in late November 1975.

Forward Exchange Contracts
1. Covering Trade Transactions
To buy or sell one's future currency commitments forward is the classic hedging method. In the most common application, a U.K. company may have a French franc import payable due in 3 months. It can cover this risk by a simple purchase of francs for the same date forward as the payment maturity, at a certain price. Forward rates are, in the final analysis, a function of the interest rate differentials of the two countries involved. Although forward premiums or discounts may apparently indicate the basic weakness or strength of a currency, they are based on the usual patterns of lower interest rates in countries with

low rates of inflation and higher rates in countries with greater inflation, weak trade balances and resultant fear of devaluation.[1] Thus, the English pound, with relatively high inflation and interest rates over the last several years, has usually been at a discount against other currencies in the forward market. This has come about since English deposit rates have been substantially higher than other countries; covering sterling deposits and also translation exposure forward by forward sales has kept the forward sterling rate under pressure.

Example G

The U.K. importer of French goods on 3 months credit with an invoice amount of FF1,000,000 may obtain the following rate quotations:

Spot rate	£1 = FF9.01
3 months forward rate	£1 = FF8.925

If the spot rate remains stable, the importer will have to put up £110,988 to purchase the French franc counterpart at maturity. On the other hand, the pound may depreciate against the franc, making his local cost considerably greater. This transaction risk can be covered by buying FF1,000,000 forward at 8.925 to coincide with the final settlement 3 months hence. In that case, the importer will have to furnish £112,045 at settlement date. No matter what happens to the franc/pound relationship, his obligation is fixed and known.

There is an implicit 'cost' in the forward premium of the franc vis-à-vis the pound in this example, but only if compared with the hypothetical outlay of the importer if the relationship between the two currencies remained unchanged. The transaction cannot be quantified, covered or uncovered, until the spot rate of the settlement date is known. The actual 'cost' could then be described. Despite the fact that not all writers accept the appellation 'cost' in such covering transactions, it is a useful concept when those future spot rates cannot be ascertained until they appear. For a certain price of £1,057 over the booked payable value, the importer has covered his risk entirely. In accounting terms the hedging difference will normally be picked up as an extra cost of sales, since the original commitment would have been booked at the cross-rate on day of invoice receipt. Upon final maturity, the importer delivers £112,045 to the bank where it has negotiated the contract and FF1,000,000 are directed to the exporter.

Cost of Forward Contracts. The 'cost' as described above of a forward exchange contract can be put into annual percentage terms for analytical purposes and comparison with other hedging methods. The premium or discount is calculated by the following simplified formula:

Example H
Calculation of forward premium/discount in percentage terms

$$\text{Discount (or premium) in \% terms} = \frac{\text{Difference in forward and spot rate}}{\text{spot rate}} \times \frac{12}{\text{months to maturity}} \times 100$$

In the French franc/sterling case above, the premium of the franc forward was:

$$= \frac{9.01 - 8.925}{9.01} \times \frac{12}{3} \times 100 = \frac{0.085}{9.01} \times 4 \times 100 = 3.77\% \text{ per annum}$$

The timing of forward coverage is important, since any delay while the local spot rate of the firm covering its risk is deteriorating may involve a higher 'cost' as opposed to the initial spot rate used for booking. For example, if interest factors remain equal and the spot rate of the pound falls to FF8.96, after 2 weeks, covering forward to the same date at a 3.77%p.a. premium would be at a rate of 8.8896, which is x in the following:

$$\left(\frac{8.96 - x}{8.96} \times \frac{12}{2.5} \times 100 \right) = 3.77\%$$

The sterling cost would then increase to £112,491 at delivery.

When forward foreign exchange rates are at a premium to local ones, the importer shows a higher local cost (in the sense of the above example); when they are at a discount it can cover future commitments at a lower cost than the spot rate, which will directly augment export income. In cases of large credit-worthy firms, no deposit will be demanded by the bank selling or buying the currency forward, although most banks impose an internal limit on the forward deals done with any one customer.

In exchange-control-free countries, there are usually no regulations for resident firms concerning forward dealings and they may undertake forward exchange commitments when and where they desire. In exchange control systems, three types of restrictions generally apply:

(a) Contracts are restricted to legitimate commercial transactions evidenced by appropriate documentation. In the strictest cases, future financial commitments in foreign currency cannot be covered forward, or contracts are limited to a final portion.
(b) Contracts must be concluded with local 'authorized' banks.
(c) The final term of any such contract is also limited, usually to match the existing limits on export or import credit terms.

An element of risk, not always considered, may now exist in the final transfer. Although a commercial firm normally puts up no money immediately and has a fixed price contract, there is a miniscule risk that the bank of negotiation may fail or suspend its dealings in the interim period before maturity (e.g. Herstatt — where the Bundesbank closed all dealings after the German side had received contractual exchange settlements but the counterpart foreign currency was not delivered abroad). In such a case, the foreign currency will not be delivered as contracted and the local exporter/importer will have to buy it directly in the spot markets, thereby bearing the same risk as if it had not covered.

Other than this, the advent of floating rates has not radically changed

the traditional forward cover framework. For normal trade transactions in the 3—6 month range, forward deals are available in all the
convertible currencies and spreads have not significantly widened.
Longer-range maturities, however, have become harder to find, and
moderately-sized deals at times tend to affect market rates more
sharply than before.

Optional-date Contracts. Not all export receipts or import payments
can be predicted with absolute certainty, or fall exactly into the
1—3—6—12 month framework. For this reason, optional-date contracts
can be considered, wherein certain currencies to be received can be sold
(or those required bought) within a maximum and minimum period in
the future. For example, a 3-month forward purchase of a foreign
currency at a premium can include an option to take down the funds
any time between the beginning and the end of the third month. Since
the bank is uncertain when such an option will be exercised, it will
charge the most unfavourable rate from the customer's point of view,
i.e. the full 3-month premium. An option sale of a currency at a
discount would include the full discount for the final option date,
although the option may be evoked earlier under terms of the deal. In
Example G, the U.K. importer might expect to pay for its imports at
any point between 2 and 3 months. The 3 month forward rate is
FF8.925 and the 2 month rate FF8.95 to the pound. An option to
effect payment at any point between 2 and 3 months would be offered
at 8.925. Exercise of the option at the beginning of month 2 would
then involve an effective differential from the spot rate of 5.66%.

$$\frac{9.01 - 8.925}{9.01} \times \frac{12}{2} \times 100 = 5.66\%$$

The technique is a useful one, but options can be negotiated in only a
few currencies, for strictly limited time periods and for commercial
reasons. The specific option desired at one point in time may not be
available.

2. Forward Contracts Covering Translation Risks
The above examples dealt with hedging external trading risks,
wherein a forward contract eliminates entirely the currency risk of
future payments or receipts. Forward contracts are also frequently used
to cover translation exposures, in which event different tax elements
arise. A U.S. parent company may consolidate the account of a U.K.
subsidiary by the monetary/non-monetary method. The net long
position in sterling to be consolidated might be £500,000 in mid-1975
when the pound is at $2.35 in the spot market. Based on a number of
considerations, the parent could decide to cover this accounting

exposure by selling pounds forward at or beyond the balance sheet closing date, which it might negotiate at $2.30 for December 31, 1975.

No actual delivery of funds need take place on December 31. Since the company is hedging balance sheet positions rather than actual transactions, it may buy pounds spot at the delivery date to fulfil its part of the deal. (Alternatively, the contract can be extended or rolled-over at a new rate.)

The spot price of the pound at that date will determine the income and tax effects to be reported. If, for instance, the pound has fallen to $2.00, the parent will show a $175,000 loss on consolidation of the net pound position of the subsidiary ($2.35 − 2.00 x 500,000), and a $150,000 gain on the forward contract ($2.30 − 2.00 x 500,000). The translation loss is not tax deductible, whereas the gain on the forward contract would be counted as ordinary income. With a full corporate tax rate in the area of 50%, the net after-tax gain on hedging is around $75,000, which will not offset the bookkeeping loss. Therefore, when hedging directly in the name of the parent, the forward contracts have to be grossed-up — taken out in larger amounts — to take account of their taxable nature. A general rule of thumb is about twice the amount of the exposed balance sheet position being hedged.[2] If such hedges can be made in a tax-free vehicle, the grossing-up necessity is eliminated.

1975 changes in tax regulations have precluded much of this ability for U.S. firms. To avoid double taxation of international business transactions carried out by U.S. companies, the U.S. has traditionally not imposed a tax on the foreign source income of a foreign corporation even if it is a 100%-owned and controlled subsidiary of a U.S. company. In very general terms, the income of that subsidiary, if fully earned abroad, is subject to U.S. tax only when remitted to the U.S. in the form of dividends.

'Sub-part F' provisions (sections 951—964 of the Internal Revenue Code of 1954) already curtailed the ability of companies to hide profits indefinitely abroad through the use of vehicle companies. Income arising in such companies since 1962 has been imputed to the U.S. parent company and taxable in the U.S., even if not declared or paid as a dividend. Until January 1976, there was still an important exception, in that foreign corporations falling under these provisions could meet a certain minimum dividend distribution requirement, so that the total income of the foreign subsidiary was not included in parent income (Section 963). This has now been revised, effective January 1, 1976, and the result is to tax all income of foreign subsidiaries which is considered 'tax haven' income. If such subsidiaries are used for hedging purposes, the profits on their forward contracts may be added to U.S. parent income and thus no longer offset translation losses on a unitary basis.

3. Hedging for Future Isolated Periods by Forward Swaps

In the major currencies and larger markets, forward exchange contracts can be negotiated not only for periods beginning with the present to some fixed maturity, but also from one future date to another. For example, a firm may wish to be covered against one currency during a period starting 3 months and ending 6 months from the present date, based on its own projected. currency positions or its perception of market trends. It would buy that currency forward for 3 months delivery, and sell it 6 months forward, thus being covered only in the desired time period.

It is similarly possible to have two simultaneous forward sale/ purchase contracts, in essence a swap, which cover the respective company for any time periods up to one year (or whatever limits the markets permit) from a date in the future, by buying a currency forward for $t - l$ periods and selling it for $t + r$. This permits both a more flexible and directed hedging policy and a reduction of hedging costs, since the cost factors involved will comprise the discount (or premium) only in the exact period covered, as shown in Example I.

Example I
Calculation of hedging costs in a swap transaction

A U.S. company wishes to cover a £1,000,000 net pound exposure in the period 3 months to 6 months from the present. It can calculate the costs of doing this as follows:

Spot pound/dollar rate	2.0305
6 months pound selling rate	1.9860 x £1,000,000 = $1,986,000
3 months pound buying rate	2.0060 x £1,000,000 = 2,006,000

Net cost of hedging in period +3 to +6 months   = $ 20,000
as opposed to a cost of hedging on a straight 6 months
forward sale of $2,030,500 − 1,986,000 or $44,500

4. Unhedging

Ungrammatical but descriptive, the term *unhedging* implies the premature closing out of a forward exchange contract before maturity, or in general, any reversing of a hedging or covering mechanism. It is not always commonly realized that the typical forward contract is not something irrevocable. In normal markets, a forward contract can be sold at any point during its existence. This can be done if the underlying reason for the hedge has changed — the position at risk eliminated — or if other exogenous factors have intervened to make the hedge superfluous.

The cost of selling a contract before maturity will be determined by market forces in the period since its inception. At times, a profit will be recorded, for instance when the devaluation (or revaluation) to be protected by the hedge has in fact already occurred. There may then be no reason to maintain a hedge with an unrealized profit (the tax impact of this is discussed in Chapter 13). Interest factors allow a calculation of the value of any given forward contract at any point in time.

Foreign Currency Loans

Where an exporter is invoicing in a currency other than its own, and which is expected to weaken, it can consider borrowing the same foreign currency for the tenor of the outstanding receivable and selling the loan proceeds spot for its own currency. At maturity, receipt of that currency will repay the borrowing. By immediately selling the loan proceeds spot at the outset for its own currency and placing them on time deposit, the ensuing interest yield will reduce the gross borrowing expense.

Example J
Hedging export proceeds by borrowing same currency

A German company has an outstanding 6 months export receivable in the amount of $500,000. It borrows that amount for 6 months at $8\frac{1}{4}\%$ p.a.

(a) It then sells $500,000 spot against Deutsche marks at
2.6150 which yields =   DM1,307,500
($500,000 x 2.6150)

(b) Interest earned on 6 months DM time deposit =   29,419
$$\left(DM1,307,500 \times 4\frac{1}{2}\% \times \frac{6}{12}\right)$$

(c) Gross DM income (a + b) =   1,336,919

(d) Interest expense on dollars = $20,625
$$\left(\$500,000 \times 8\frac{1}{4}\% \times \frac{6}{12}\right)$$
Since this will be paid at the end of 6 months, it is bought
forward against marks at 2.5980 (6 months forward rate)
at a cost of   53,584

(e) Net pre-tax revenue at end of transaction   DM1,283,335

Had it sold the dollars forward originally at the 6 months forward rate of 2.5940, the net receipt at maturity would have been DM1,297,000.

($500,000 x 2.5940 = DM1,297,000)

Normally, the foreign currency borrowing technique should equal roughly the cost of a forward contract, under the interest parity theory.[3] Bank spreads and local reserve requirements may result in cost differentials, as above.

Discounting Foreign Currency Receivables

Export bills denominated in foreign currency can usually be discounted in local markets, exchange controls allowing this as an aid to exporters. The bank discounting such currency bills will itself apply a mixture of the domestic rate and the net cost/yield of the swap transaction. Since, however, the local interest cost, affected also by minimum reserve requirements, may differ from the Euro-market rates underlying that theory, the net revenue can be slightly lower or higher than that resulting from a straightforward forward contract.

This technique is not possible in many exchange control-based countries, where foreign currency borrowings are permitted only under strict limitation, or not at all.

Example K

Discounting foreign currency receivables

In the same German example, the exporter has received $500,000 of discountable 6 month trade bills drawn on the importer.

(a) These are discounted at $7^9/16\%$ p.a. at a net interest cost of $18,906, leaving a dollar principal amount of $481,074

(b) The dollar proceeds are sold at spot at 2.6150, yielding   DM1,258,009

(c) Assuming again that the primary purpose of the transaction was to eliminate the currency risk and the funds are not needed for local purposes, they would be placed in a 6 month DM time deposit at $4\frac{1}{2}\%$ p.a. This would yield interest of   <u>28,305</u>

    Net pre-tax revenue   DM1,286,314

Lines for such transactions can be set up with the company's bank in advance and generally carry a commitment fee.

Foreign Currency Accounts

For companies with two-way flows of the same currency which are perhaps unpredictable and sporadic — but have an offsetting ability at least in mathematical terms — the use of a foreign currency account should be considered. These are permitted either generally under certain conditions or specifically on a case-to-case basis by the respective exchange controls of most countries.

If a U.K. company has both dollar income and dollar outflows, it may obtain permission from the Bank of England to receive and maintain them in a *currency 'hold' account* in dollars at a U.K. bank, thus overriding the standard regulation to convert all currency receipts immediately to sterling. In exceptional cases, this permission can even be extended to allow *'retained currency' accounts* at banks abroad, which have the same purpose. The normal justification for such a permission is a roughly matching inflow and outflow of the currency in question over predictable periods in the future, with no more than one month's requirement of that currency to be lodged in the account on average.

While these accounts are specifically authorized to save administrative and particularly conversion costs for the exporter, they represent an implicit hedge against import payables, as otherwise export receipts are immediately brought back into the local currency. The hedge could be as high as the amount of one month's income by currency. In some markets, interest at Euro-rates can be negotiated and paid on such accounts.

Foreign Currency Bought, Held in Deposit Until Payment

An analogous risk-avoiding possibility for importers owing foreign currency is to borrow their own currency, use the proceeds to buy the foreign currency spot and place the funds on deposit (where permitted). This again can be worked out on a straight-cost basis, using a $500,000 import into Germany.

Example L
Covering import risks by foreign currency borrowing

(a)   The importer borrows DM1,308,000 at 5¾%
       ($500,000 × 2.6160)

(b)   The loan proceeds are used to buy $500,000 spot which are placed in a 6 months time deposit yielding 7¼%. This yields interest of $18,125.

$$\left(\$500,000 \times 7.25\% \times \frac{6}{12} \right)$$

(c)   The interest is sold forward at 6 months which at maturity will yield   DM47,016
       ($18,125 × 2.5940)

(d)   The interest cost on the DM loan is   37,605

$$\left(DM1,308,000 \times 5\tfrac{3}{4}\% \times \frac{6}{12} \right)$$

(e)   Net gain on hedging transaction   DM9,411

The importer would have booked the dollar payable at DM1,308,000 at the spot rate of invoice date. The gain on the above transaction would reduce the net local cost of goods to DM1,298,589. Had it simply bought the dollars forward directly, the outlay at settlement date would have been DM1,299,000 ($500,000 × 2.5980). Again, dealing in two independent markets shows different cost elements which should be analysed before one of several hedging methods is chosen.

The biggest constraint here could be the company's banks, which may be unwilling to lend local currency for 'unproductive' purposes, particularly when any credit restrictions are in force. Many central banks also prohibit such transactions.

Factoring

Where an exporter is selling on open account and therefore receives no discountable bills, it is possible to assign the actual receivables as collateral for related bank financing. Both commercial banks and specialized factoring institutions in certain countries offer factoring facilities to accomplish this.

It is possible to factor receivables denominated in foreign currency, as well as those in local units. The equivalent local value of the receivables is then advanced to the exporter until maturity. Here the costs involved are the commercial risk factor, the cost of financing (if required) and the exchange risk coverage (related to the forward rate, since this is not automatically included in the transaction). Factoring thus tends to be a higher priced way of obtaining financing against foreign receivables, rather than a hedging mechanism.

Leasing

A less-used hedging method for the export of capital goods is leasing. For marketing reasons, an exporter of capital goods may not be able to bill in his own currency nor wish to receive an importer's weak currency. It may consider selling the goods outright to a leasing company in the country of the importer, which leases them on to the ultimate user. Neither side then has an exchange risk, and the exporter is paid immediately. While attractive in certain cases, particularly in long-term contracts on which forward cover may be difficult, it is not always easy to arrange a tripartite arrangement covering all the legal and fiscal considerations between seller, leasing company and buyer/lessee.

Exchange Risk Guarantees

Even the above wide range of external risk hedging techniques does not cover every eventuality, since exchange and banking markets are neither perfect nor long-term in orientation. For this reason, several governments have established exchange risk guarantee (ERG) programmes to add to the flexibility of exporters. Japan, for example, began a programme in 1975 offering insurance to exporters for losses incurred when a foreign currency involved in an export contract depreciates by 3% or more in relation to the yen after the contract is signed. Currencies covered by that insurance include the pound sterling, the French franc, the Deutsche mark and the U.S. dollar. The insurance is applicable to contracts for the export of aircraft, ships, railroad rolling stock and certain other industrial equipment after a period of 2—15 years. Switzerland's Foreign Trade Ministry created a similar programme in 1974.

These programmes are usually found in hard currency countries where exporters of industrial equipment sell under long-term contracts and where traditional short-term cover is not available or appropriate.

Summary of Limitations on External Techniques

Banking policy, market limitations and/or exchange control regulations will constrain or prohibit the use of these techniques in many instances. Not all methods will always be available to any company, nor will all be equally advantageous. The appropriateness and cost of each should be part of the normal managerial analysis when setting an exposure strategy, which is the subject of the next chapter.

Notes

1. The supply/demand forces in the forward exchange markets, including those arising from interest differentials, are analysed in many studies, among which are: Einzig, Paul, *A Dynamic Theory of Forward Exchange*, Second Edition, London: Macmillan, 1967 and Wasserman, Prindl and Townsend, *International Money Management*, New York: American Management Association, 1972, Chapter 7.
2. Even practitioners disagree about the grossing-up effect. See Curtis, David, 'Hedging balance sheet exposure after tax', *Euromoney*, April 1975, and Chown, Kelen and Marechal, 'Hedging balance sheet exposure after tax — a reply', *Euromoney*, June 1975.
3. The interest parity theory deals with the differential between spot and forward rates of exchange, explaining that this is a function of the interest rates in any two currencies. The buying/selling of forward exchange to take advantage of covered interest arbitrage possibilities between two currencies will quickly bring back the forward/spot rates to a position of equilibrium. See the same references given in Note 1.

CHAPTER 9

Setting Hedging Strategy

The appropriate strategy for dealing with foreign exchange risks is derived from the overall corporate objectives of the company. For most firms, the primary objective will be the maximization of earnings expressed in terms of the currency of the parent. Others will wish to protect assets, sales or market share at all costs. Depending upon the perceived corporate objective, the attitude of any one company towards accepting or avoiding risks other than those involved in its basic production/sales/finance structure will evolve. From that attitude to risk, the individual strategy of covering all, some or none of the exchange risk inherent in an international configuration will be established. If the firm considers its primary objective to be the maximization of sales income from home and foreign operations and is otherwise adverse to risk-taking, it may well wish to cover both translation and economic risks completely. If, on the other hand, the firm sees exchange gains as an additional component of income or determines that the cost of being fully covered outweighs the potential negative effects of any exchange rate movement, it may establish a currency-by-currency strategy resulting in a policy to cover certain positions fully, but to leave others either partially or completely uncovered.

Deciding What Should Be Hedged

For the exporting/importing firm, a decision to hedge all exchange risks is a typical and appropriate strategy. Either exporters or importers may have currency commitments which cannot be changed or avoided. The exporting company may be requested to invoice in a currency other than its own or it may do so for marketing reasons. The importing company will often be forced to accept foreign currency contracts denominated in either the supplier's or a third currency.

Such transactions will then have to be brought back to a neutral point by hedging of one type or another, if the firm wishes to eliminate all exchange exposure.

The firm wishing to be fully protected against exchange risk may take the attitude that it is engaged in trading, that its expertise lies in marketing and/or manufacturing and that it wants to bear no avoidable risks. It will sell or buy its currency commitments forward, discount or even factor its receivables, borrow foreign currency or use whatever other method is equally effective and least costly. For example, making an analysis of all the external techniques in Examples J and K (Chapter 8) would compare the relevant hedging costs for its dollar receivables with 6 months maturity to ascertain the net pre-tax revenue, as follows:

Example M

	Net DM revenue after hedge
Forward sale of dollars	1,297,000
Discount of dollar trade bills	1,286,314
Dollar borrowing, spot purchase of marks, short term Deutsche mark deposit	1,283,397

In this case, it would opt for the forward sale of dollars. Rate structures at different times could, of course, make either of the other two options more advantageous.

The policy of risk coverage may be determined in part by sales margins. In some industries, sales margins may be minute, so that even the forward premiums and discounts, which tend to range around 2—5% or more on an annualized basis for periods under one year, may seriously affect profits. These firms need to examine billing policies and marketing constraints to see whether internal measures, such as changing the currency of billing, are not a more acceptable alternative.

The attitude of the company's management to risk is the other determinant factor. In the previous example, the amount at risk was $500,000. The German exporter might calculate that there is a 60% chance that the dollar will depreciate 1% against the German mark in the next 6 months (and a 40% chance that there will be no change). The expected monetary loss is therefore:

$$\$500,000 \times 0.60 \times 0.01 = \$3,000 \text{ in mark equivalents, or}$$
$$\text{DM7,850 @ 2.6150}$$

A direct forward sale of dollars will bring in DM1,297,000 with certainly, whereas the above analysis shows that the probable uncovered outcome would result in a receipt of about DM1,300,000. (The receivables will have been booked as DM1,307,500, using the spot rate of 2.6150. The probable outcome if no action is taken is expected to reduce that amount by DM10,460 to DM1,299,650.) Hedging by the least expensive means will result in a diminution of sales proceeds of DM10,500. Here the risk-adverse company would take the less risky course of hedging; a more aggressive firm might remain uncovered.

In many cases, the expected probable outcome of loss (X) will roughly equal the cost of hedging (Y); the attitude of the firm to risk may foster its acceptance of a risk which is apparently equal to the cost of hedging.

In Bretton Woods days, many companies were prepared to remain largely uncovered, except in extreme and sporadic cases. Their reasoning was two-fold; under a system of fixed rates and narrow bands, parity changes of material proportion were few and often predictable. The central banks were committed to supporting the spot value of their currency within those bands, often supporting forward rates as well, as in the well-known 1967 case of sterling. The cost to a company of completely hedging over time would thus outweigh the occasional exchange losses from devaluation/revaluation even if the latter were never covered. This type of 'self-insurance' against risk is now rarely practised, given the very large swings in rates and the unpredictability of their magnitude or timing.

Multinational Companies

For the international firm with subsidiaries, the hedging problem is more complex. Its risks are of different kinds and at different locations. To remain completely covered against all risks may be costly and sometimes impossible. Certain countries either do not provide forward market coverage possibilities (South America) or have local borrowing cost structures which are inordinately high in terms of the actual perceived risks. Strategy in this context is based on a currency-by-currency analysis of the risks inherent in each position, ascertaining the probable outcome, and comparing this to the individual costs of covering each currency position. This may still mean coverage of all risks in many cases.

For certain firms, the result of that analysis may be covering only *transaction risks*, i.e. when actual conversions and thus realized loss to the group may occur. This includes covering all local conversion exposures of the subsidiaries affected, dividends declared and payable to the parent and export/import transactions at headquarters level. It will involve covering of future expected profit flows in certain cases, even though these have not yet been achieved.

Covering transaction exposure only means that translation gains or losses may still arise; firms with such a policy must accept them or engage in additional hedging costs. Example N shows one case of a subsidiary covering its transactional exposures with direct implications for the parent.

Example N
Effect of covering a subsidiary's transaction exposure

Assume a U.S. parent with only one consolidated subsidiary, located in France. The latter's balance sheet is as follows:

(French franc million equivalents)

	FF	£	Lit.		FF	DM
Cash	30					
Accounts receivable	20	30	10	Accounts payable	20	20
Inventory	20			Other current	10	
Current Assets	110			Current Liabilities	50	
Fixed assets	180			Long-term debt	140	
				Equity	100	
Total assets	290			Total liabilities	290	

The transaction risk of the subsidiary is comprised of its lire and sterling receivables and its Deutsche mark payables. The French franc exposure to the group on consolidation, using the temporal method, consists of:

Plus		Minus	
Cash	30	Accounts payable	20
Accounts receivable	20	Other current	10
		Long-term debt	140
	50		170

or a net position of FF120 million short. If the French subsidiary hedges its current risks by forward contracts in sterling, lire and Deutsche mark, its franc position to be consolidated becomes FF100 million short, an appreciable change for the parent company.

Cash	30	Accounts payable	40
Accounts receivable	60	Other current	10
		Long-term debt	140
	90		190

Comparison of Risk and Hedging Costs

To carry out the analysis underlying a hedge/no hedge strategy, the appropriate policy is:

1. examine the possible impact of all types of risk on an individual currency basis;
2. decide which are unacceptable;
3. hedge these with the least expensive means of protection. This strategy will force the firm first to look at internal measures, where expected costs may be lower than external ones. All hedging measures have a cost, whether easily discernible or not, and many have regulatory restrictions as well.

A firm might undertake the following analysis, when its present translation exposure in French francs is calculated to be FF10,000,000 long (following the compilation of information from its reporting systems). This position is not forecast to change appreciably, nor is there any material economic exposure not represented by the accounting data. Other currency exposures are minimal.

Analysis of rate forecasts shows that the French franc is predicted to depreciate by 10% in the accounting period under review. This would result in a translation loss to the parent of $200,000. The management concludes that this:

(a) must be reported as an extraordinary charge to income,
(b) would reduce net income by 20%, and
(c) is therefore unacceptable if the loss can be avoided by hedging at significantly lower cost.

Determining the Most Suitable Methods

One of the most difficult problems then arises: selection of the most appropriate methods to achieve the desired position at the lowest projected cost. The company may be able to use both internal methods as well as external ones; both should be considered.

1. Leading Payments Out of France

Its review might begin with the adjustment of intercompany accounts due to or from France. Since the goal is to reduce net assets in France, the subsidiary could be requested to accelerate its payments to the parent or the latter could delay payments to France. The leading/ lagging actions will have a direct cost to the leading subsidiary (France) and an opportunity gain to the receiving or lagging entity (U.S.). The quantifiable cost factors are the interest paid, or foregone, by the French subsidiary and the interest yield of the recipient, if those funds can in fact be put to use. Lagging payments due to France from the parent or other subsidiary whose currency is expected to remain stable, has the same equivalent costs.

As explained directly, either leading or lagging will be controlled to some extent by the French exchange control authorities and often the other affiliate's country and this may limit the range of that technique.

2. Assets or Liability Adjustment

Given time in which to adjust the French balance sheet structure, the firm may be able to reduce the cash, short-term investments or inventory (if defined as exposed) of the subsidiary. This technique also has cost elements: foregone interest on surplus liquidity, possible loss of production or sales if inventory is below working needs; these expenses could then be very large. However, if executed as a short-term tactic before an imminent French franc depreciation, costs may be minimal.

3. Advance Settlement of Third Party Payables

The rationale here would again be to shift French balance sheet positions to reduce its actual exposure. The accelerated settlement of its import payables in a harder currency, normally possible, has costs in that liquidity must be reduced or borrowings increased to fund the pre-payment.

Other anticipatory methods, such as changing the currency of billing of the French subsidiary are too long-term in nature to be used to counter a short-term French franc risk. They would be considered viable only in cases where there is time for those techniques to reduce the French franc and increase the foreign currency assets of the subsidiary.

External techniques available to protect translation exposure would include primarily:

1. Forward sale of French francs by the parent.
2. Creation of additional French franc liabilities, either in the name of the subsidiary or of the parent. In both cases, the French francs borrowed would have to be converted into dollars or some other currency expected to remain stable before rate changes occur.

Cost Comparison

After all appropriate methods have been studied and their cost ascertained, the treasurer can develop a comparative table showing the costs of each internal and external technique (Figure 18).

Figure 18. Table of hedging methods and costs

	Expected cost	Cost basis
Leading/lagging	α	French subsidiary borrowing cost for x months less interest yield on dollars or other currency
Asset reduction	β	Loss of yield on investments
Premature settlement of French subsidiary's payables	τ	Financing cost
Borrowing French francs	δ	Domestic or Euro-French francs borrowing rate (less possible yield on foreign currency deposit)
Forward sale of francs	ϵ	Forward market rate
Remaining totally uncovered	$200,000	

With the knowledge of present and future positions, the potential impact on the firm, the firm's own attitude to risk and the cost of each covering technique, the decision to cover the French franc risk deemed unacceptable becomes a mathematical one.[1] Covering a number of risks in different currencies would involve a separate but similar analysis for each one.

Carrying Out the Corporate Response

An organizational element enters in the implementation of hedging policy. The financial office will decide the hedging techniques to be used; at or before this point, top management will need to be informed of the extent of risk, the extent of hedging and the cost/risk analysis which went into the decision. In some cases, top management will determine the strategy directly. The best approach is to have a foreign exchange committee, comprised of representatives from treasury, controller, tax and possibly marketing sections, which reviews the scope of the treasury's recommendations.[2] The alternative is to lodge foreign exchange risk responsibility in one individual who makes the analysis and recommendations under the control of the chief finance officer.

The execution of hedging transactions is a practical one, based on the nature of the risk to be covered and where the coverage effect in financial terms is to be recorded. The necessity for hedging of local items matching actual exposure of the affiliates to be carried out at affiliate level has already been pointed out. Here, the offsetting hedge will have no equivalent effect unless entered directly into by the subsidiary and appearing in its own books. In most cases, the subsidiary will also have to deal in its local markets with authorized banks; exchange control systems are very strict in this regard. The guidelines under which subsidiaries operate must be strictly determined: the timing, banks used and maturities may all need to be directed.

With translation exposure, the treasurer has more flexibility to carry out the designated response. The large corporation is able to deal in a number of markets virtually simultaneously. It will gather quotations from various sources, having over time ascertained which banks or traders are most helpful and which offer the best rates on various currencies or deals. Depending on the local exchange control rules of the parent, hedging will be carried out on a global basis.

Implementation, like good identification, requires a logical and structured system, wherein the responsibilities of each official and each location are made clear. Individual action by any one subsidiary cannot be optimal, and should not be allowed (see the third case study in Chapter 10). The requisite centralization recommended for the identification and analysis areas is again necessary in the implementation of hedging tactics.

Notes

1. An elegant mathematical description of the simple hedging decision is found in Shapiro and Rutenberg, 'When to hedge against devaluation', *Managerial Science*, August 1974.
2. For descriptions of approaches used by 3 major companies see:
   Ankrom, Robert K., 'Top level approach to the foreign exchange problem', *Harvard Business Review*, July—August 1974 (Chrysler); Hoyt, Newton H. Jr., 'The management of currency exchange risk by the Singer Company', *Financial Management*, Spring 1972; Schotanus, Eugene L., 'A strategy for coping with exchange risks', *Management Accounting*, January 1971 (Deere).

CHAPTER 10

Centralization versus Decentralization – Three case studies

This chapter presents three examples of the ways in which multinationals have approached the exchange management problem. The basic policies are: strong centralization of the finance function with a detailed underlying reporting system, decentralization under strict parameters from the parent and at least as developed reporting, and decentralization without particular guidelines for the subsidiaries. The examples illustrate and confirm the author's view that only centralization in the first or second formats is adequate to control this complex field. All three policies can be found in myriad other companies and countries; for obvious reasons, the actual firms are left unidentified. Each is a company with worldwide sales in multimillion dollar amounts.

Full Centralization

The first example concerns a large consumer durable company, characterized by strong financial management, concentrated at the parent level, and an expansive reporting system. Its philosophy has been to direct top management's attention to exchange positions and for them to share and ultimately approve the finance department's perception of risk. This company embodies most of the principles outlined in this text. Its exchange management approach is closely integrated with tax and liquidity management policy, the latter being seen as part of the same managerial problem. It identifies both the transaction and the translation risks in its worldwide operations; both are considered equally necessary to ascertain and control.

Its reporting system is detailed in both accounting and treasury terms and anticipatory. Emphasis is given to forecasting all types of exposure by currency. The critical positions of each major group member: cash, short-term investments and borrowings are cabled daily to the central office, read into the computer and compiled for the treasurer's review the next morning.

Local input as to both external and internal constraints is massive. For example, parameters of cost and exchange control affecting leading and lagging are reported weekly. An internal economist's department supplies the treasury with macro-economic data and short-term rate forecasts (upper and lower expected ranges for rate movements in various periods).

Decision-making has been fully concentrated at the head office, where the finance department includes some 40 managers and analysts. Subsidiaries are rarely consulted as to strategy, under the assumption that massive and frequent data make all risks and alternatives apparent.

A European vehicle company is utilized to carry out transactions of a wide-ranging nature (among others, long-term financing and export financing). It has had no senior officers of its own (until recently) and is not party to the strategic or practical decisions.

Foreign subsidiaries are generally passive; they carry out such hedging tactics as the parent directs and do not have fully fledged international treasurers as local finance managers except in one instance. Policy-setting covers a wide number of alternatives; forward contracts are in some respects the last alternatives to be considered. The company has, for example, evolved an extended programme of leading or lagging its large-scale intercompany transactions. This is again based on an extensive data input and short-term internal rate projections. Part of the deliberation here is to compare the borrowing costs of both payer and payee, giving a cost parameter for credit term adjustment with the cost or yield aspects of direct forward cover. Only when the latter has an appreciable advantage over the former, or if leading/lagging under expected cross-rates has too high an uncertainty range, are forward contracts taken out.

Coupled with a flexible range of covering methods is a generally conservative policy towards risk. Senior non-financial management is party to the overall strategy decision, which normally is hedging unacceptable translation risks and attempting to minimize the economic risks not arising directly in consolidation. Centralization is fostered by the use of the reinvoicing vehicle company, which to a large extent can take transaction risk from local subsidiaries by buying from or selling to them in their local currencies. Forward contracts are placed only by the parent with its own house banks, although these are made on behalf of foreign affiliates where appropriate.

This system is a vigorous and well-developed one, found in many similar cases, particularly in the very large European companies which are already multinationals of long standing. It is based on full centralization, since decentralization of the finance function has never taken place and clear responsibility for exchange gains/losses is lodged at the treasurer's level. An excellent, if expensive, reporting system is its complement, one which allows little chance of overlooking risks or any alternatives to cover them. Local input is widespread, but statistical, rather than managerial. The centralization of the finance function might be criticized in that it leaves little to the discretion of local personnel. (The motivational problems which could arise here are discussed in Chapter 14.) In general, though, the finance function is one of the ablest of management control in the company, and its development is mirrored in its foreign exchange information and policy-setting systems.

Decentralization Under Strong Guidelines and Communications

The second example is of a primary products producer which has developed a policy of 'guided decentralization'. It has worldwide interests, but the largest international transactions are either in Europe, or between Europe and the production subsidiaries on one hand and Europe and the parent country on the other. While it is divisionalized in marketing, the finance function cuts across these lines and assumes direct responsibility for financial management questions.

The latter are decentralized in that a competent European headquarters operation exists, with a 20-man financial staff embodying treasury, tax and accounting responsibilities. The head of the finance group is an assistant treasurer of the parent company, with commensurate authority and signing power.

The function of the latter group is to act as the 'eyes and ears' of the group in Europe (there is a similar Asian headquarters), to provide local input and undertake local exchange contracts, and particularly to act as a catalyst and sounding board in group decision-making.

The reporting system of this company is strongly developed and directed to the treasury function. Both the parent treasurer and the European treasurer receive the financial statements, projections and budgets of the respective subsidiaries as soon as prepared. Well-trained area finance directors, each covering several countries, complement the local staffs.

The local finance managers, who tend to be accountants, report both to their local manager as far as preparation of statements and local cash management are concerned and to the headquarters units for the larger financial considerations affecting the group. There are constant verbal communications and visits between local officials and the European headquarters, which acts as a link to the U.S. parent.

The reporting system, however, is less fully developed than in the previous case. While it requires a number of cash and sales forecasts, some of the local operations provide poor and sketchy data in this area. A complete banking relationship/credit line usage reporting system is still lacking.

Economic exposure is identified, in that many local sales affiliates act only as a conduit for imports into their local market. It is felt that local price structures cannot be changed within 6 months, so that if the foreign price of an imported product increases, or the local currency depreciates, the subsidiary in question is exposed to loss during that period.

The communication between parent and European headquarters is instructive. The determination of exchange risk is done jointly on the basis of full currency reports and projections (a problem here is that these reports can take up to 30 days to complete and send to the two centres). The two staff groups communicate their individual rate projections, analyse hedging possibilities and come to a mutual decision as to coverage of translation or other risks for the corporation on a weekly basis. Standard policy is to be neutral in translation risk, unless there is a natural 'positive' position in currencies likely to move in only one direction against the parent currency. Therefore, all corporate balance sheet risks (and all dividends) are covered with the occasional exceptions of short sterling or long Deutsche mark positions.

Actual hedging is chiefly undertaken in Europe by the headquarters staff. After a long trial, it was concluded that:

(1) Rates in the U.S. markets did not vary appreciably from those obtainable by the group at the same point in time in London, Zurich, Frankfurt, etc.;

(2) Because of time differentials and the necessity to have continual local bank contacts, hedging was slightly more effective to carry out in Europe; and

(3) The off-shore finance function could place the hedges more easily in non-tax-paying subsidiaries.

Thus, the hedging of translation risk is decentralized after central discussion and decision-making.

One area where the European staff has not yet convinced the parent of the need for further decentralized decisions is in economic exposure areas. The European staff has recommended that the local exposures described above during the 6-month period necessary for price adjustment should also be fully covered, but this has not been approved by the parent, which has ordained that only translation exposures be hedged. This is a source of continued debate.

Hedging is not limited to forward contracts alone. The weekly strategy-setting process considers the timing and extent of product price changes, the direct action possible on intercompany payables and receivables and third party payables, the various implications of financing techniques for both exposure and funding needs and the choice of vehicles to be used for absorption of costs. A detailed specific strategy follows.

Local affiliates have little part in the hedging decision, although they do report on local market conditions, rates and restrictions. When hedging must literally be effected through forward contracts in the name of the subsidiaries, they are instructed to move the counterpart local currency to the bank or correspondent bank with whom the headquarters has done the deal. They may also be requested to make intercompany loans, to accept loans, or to draw-down or build-up liquidity as part of overall strategy. Internal management accounting is designed to hold them blameless for local financial results thereby impaired, by eliminating financial charges and exchange adjustment from management reports (some criticism is levied in that preparation for such shifting of assets is often abrupt).

This type of decentralization implies a broadening of the financial function to include more personnel, better local input and discussion with a bridging of time zones and distance. It has many advantages which even the well-structured system of case one may lack: a deeper and closer knowledge of local risks and alternatives is the most apparent of these. The regular exposure analysis procedures bring together different viewpoints and experiences. The motivation of each manager and his training are stressed and a certain esprit de corps, not always apparent in multinationals, would appear to permeate the group.

The company seems to have excellent control over its liquidity and financing relationships. An outsider would conclude that the former was excessive in amount, in the sense of a trustee maintaining the capital entrusted to him, but this is a philosophical point. Cash management is integrated in the same structure: there is the same input and discussion of cash management techniques, where these are not mechanical and automatic. A netting system, for example, is run by the European group and eliminates more than 50% of the relevant inter-company payments and conversions.

Publicly reported exchange losses have nevertheless occurred; the company has long-standing large-term borrowings in Swiss francs and Deutsche marks, which have not been fully covered and which have resulted in sporadic losses as those currencies appreciated against the dollar. The decision to draw-down credits in hard currencies was made with that potential at least partly in mind and with comparison of the present value of the lower interest cost. (At the time of borrowing the company also had Swiss franc and Deutsche mark income from local operations in those countries, which partially offset the appreciation of the loans.)

As an operational structure, this type of decentralization can be seen to improve and deepen financial controls in a fragmented world. There is a feeling of constant questioning, evaluation and communication which this structure fosters. The interchange of personnel and ideas strengthens the group and makes the frequent visits of financial personnel more efficient. Such an approach to the exchange management process is an excellent one and the best of the three examples in this chapter. The costs of the European headquarters, as far as better financial management can be quantified, are far outweighed by the benefits of fuller understanding, better strategy, cash management savings and losses not incurred.

Decentralization

The last example deals with a consumer products company with a strong expansion in Europe. Over the last decade, it has developed both manufacturing and sales affiliates in a number of European and South American locations. Basically one-product oriented by tradition, its attempts to diversify at home by acquisition led to a number of direct investments, creating new divisions and new foreign subsidiaries in only partially related industries.

The treasury function at the parent level was traditionally small — less than 10 managers — with a great deal of autonomy left to the individual divisions and their controllers. There was and is neither an international division nor an international treasurer; foreign exchange risks were never clearly the responsibility of any one group. Marketing factors were often critical in any case — the company made its original reputation in this area — and marketing managers themselves were directly involved in hedging decisions without treasury input.

There were no regional headquarters, although the European sales and asset structure alone exceeded $100 million and would have warranted such a headquarters function. There was little or no contact between the subsidiaries of different divisions in one country; even subsidiaries of the same division had minimal written and virtually no personal communication.

The reporting system reflected this fragmentation. Reports were first made divisionally from the local controllers to their divisional managers and only thereafter passed on to the central treasury. The divisions in the home country themselves were located in various major cities; an appreciable delay resulted in the reporting process until the treasurer received the balance sheet data from each subsidiary, which in any case had major weakness in detail and currency breakdown. Forecasting concentrated on sales and profits: a very elaborate system for predicting those flows for each product group and comparing budget estimates with actuals was involved, but this gave little insight into future exposure risks or liquidity positions. Being in general in very volatile markets and usually underestimating sales, the company's budgeted projections were at great variance from actual events and proved of minimal value to the treasurer in anticipating risks. Separate currency projection was not included in the budgets.

Responsibility for exchange risk management was unclear. The treasury nominally had the task to cover the corporation's translation exposures. Since the local affiliates mainly served their own domestic markets and there were few exports (although some intercompany trade existed), translation risks tended to be based on the company's net working capital positions in each country using the current/non-current convention. These, as well as anticipated yearly dividends, were continually covered forward from the head office under a philosophy of offsetting all translation risks. Foreign exchange contracts, usually to coincide with the fiscal year end, were taken out in the New York market.

This standard policy was obscured, however, by independent action of marketing personnel. To the extent they understood exchange exposure, various attempts were made on a divisional basis to transfer assets to hard currency countries and liabilities into soft currencies, particularly in the divisions where some intercompany trade existed. This was done idiosyncratically by divisional managers. A somewhat unique pricing and fee structure allowed further asset adjustment under the direction of the division managers/controllers. Since the management evaluation system was also divisionalized, with exchange gains and interest income accruing directly to the various divisions, there was considerable motivation to take or cover positions in the market in the name of local entities without consideration of the group effect.

Local subsidiaries were free to control their own liquidity and exchange risks within a wide degree of latitude. The more aggressive finance personnel would either independently hedge their local exposures (particularly arising from imports) or lead and lag payments bilaterally with other members of the same division. As a natural human tendency, the stronger, more experienced or more dynamic managers tended to show better performances. In sleepier divisions, little local action was taken. In one division, economic exposure was increased in an unforeseen way by a rigid billing policy. Products from the parent company were invoiced in dollars to U.K. sales subsidiaries, which re-exported the same products with sterling invoices. A needless pound exposure was added to the group and an economic exposure unrelated to marketing factors was created for the U.K. side, since the product involved had low price elasticity of demand.

This is a classic case of the potential problems of decentralization, poor responsibility setting and inadequate reporting. Surprisingly, the company did not suffer particularly from these deficiencies and has reported no major exchange losses in recent years. It had certain natural advantages, in major sales and assets in hard currency countries, which gave it an automatic net long position in those currencies to offset potential losses in others It was in a strong sales upswing in the early 1970s, with high margins and relatively price-inelastic product groups. The lack of recognizing risks in the future or ascertaining economic exposure never became acute. The parent remained more or less covered against its more significant exposures, even if its exchange management was far from optimal.

The real cost of such policies to this group came in the form of opportunity profits foregone. Major exchange losses were not reported, but better management could easily have realized exchange gains without speculation, given its natural currency positions. A priori, its tax policy could hardly be optimal, given the same weaknesses. And clear opportunity costs were borne in many other areas of International

Money Management. The company possessed very massive liquidity in one division in Europe. This was mainly placed on time deposits with local banks, much of it in sterling. While interest income in that division was high, it did not necessarily reflect the maximum possible yield from both interest and capital appreciation if deployed more strategically. For example, in 1973, almost £3,000,000 of sterling was being kept in short-term deposits, although the risk of sterling depreciation was not inconsiderable.

Furthermore, there were several countries in which two, three or four divisions had subsidiaries. There was no contact on the intracountry level. They dealt with different banks, had different credit lines and reported to different managers. In the worst cases, one subsidiary in a country had liquidity invested in short-term holdings, while one or more affiliates in the same country were borrowing at much higher rates. The lack of pooling cost the group the differential between those two rates, as did the more exceptional cases of local subsidiaries each hedging types of exposures which were mutually offsetting. As can be imagined, mechanical cash management systems were also inadequate.

Over time, these problems have become more apparent; the company has created a European cash manager to control liquidity, direct cash management and coordinate exposure management on that continent. The reporting systems are being improved; responsibility for exchange gains/losses (and direct attribution of them) has been clearly given to the finance department. Assuming that the company becomes less liquid over time, a logical next step will be to give responsibility and credit for interest earned/paid to the finance function, probably making it into an independent profit centre. Concomitant action will be to deny subsidiaries the right to lead/lag or to hedge without parent or European headquarters approval. Over time it is likely that this company will move closer to the policies of case two.

Dozens of similar cases of decentralization involving inefficiency and poor risk management could be cited. Typically, many firms which are advantageously decentralized in marketing, research or production carry that philosophy through to the finance function, often creating bigger weaknesses than those in this example. Considered arguments are often heard concerning the virtues of financial decentralization and the use of local personnel to solve local problems directly. None of these ring true and none work efficiently, in the author's experience. They presuppose an impossibly broad knowledge of group problems on the part of local officials, and in general, an expertise which they have not gathered and for which they are neither properly trained nor evaluated. The sum of such a whole is less than its parts, in that an optimal strategy for the group and its independent parts cannot possibly be expected. This exacerbates the very fragmentation which a coherent exchange management policy seeks to dispel.

CHAPTER 11

Application of Mathematical/Computer Techniques

Characteristic for exchange exposure management are complexity, uncertainty and often immense quantities of data. In all of these areas, the use of mathematical techniques and computers are being considered, but are still in a rudimentary stage.

Computer Utilization

Computer application in the field so far has tended to be successful at three levels:

Communications/data base storage;
Risk identification programs;
Simple models to project currency risks or the effects of currency changes in the future.

Communications and Data Storage

The computer can serve as a communications link between departments of the firm and between various affiliates. Market information such as spot and forward rate quotations can be monitored and visibly reported. More importantly, perhaps, the nature of present computers is such that these can maintain a data base of virtually unlimited size on the company's structure, flows and risks. Such information, updated continually, then serves as the basis for analytic models of all types.

Data-Processing Programs (Risk Identification)

The quantity of data to be assimilated and the time necessary to process them have often hindered the identification of risks and their potential impact. Delay factors at the local level in closing financial statements are only part of the process; reports are gathered worldwide, sent to the parent or headquarters location and eventually consolidated, analysed or projected. Until recently, this has been a manual/semi-mechanical process with a median delay of 30—45 days after month-end closing being standard before a company could identify even its historical exposures. Often the treasury has had to wait for all reports from major subsidiaries to trickle in from abroad before the processing of total information can take place.

Computer programs can handle this problem extremely efficiently and at low cost. Balance sheets and similar information can be sent in by cable, read by peripheral equipment into a data base and called up at will. One such program takes up to 100 balance sheets in up to 50 currencies. It can produce different print-outs with very little cost, so that the various programs can be run each time a new balance sheet arrives, rather than waiting for all data. This particular system allows the treasury to call up:

1. The present consolidated position of the group by currency;
2. The future position of the group by currency in various time periods (based on budgets, not projections within the model; this requires other techniques);
3. The locations where a currency is held/owed;
4. The assets in which a currency is held/owed;
5. The non-local currency risk of any subsidiary (i.e. its transaction exposure);
6. All off-balance-sheet items (hedges, leases, etc.) with their book and present valuation.

The program replaces the same arithmetic calculations done manually. Sub-programs bring in tax effects, exchange control limitations and the opportunity to net intercompany positions. By adding other information on company financial transactions, data-processing programs assist in integrating liquidity management with exchange risk, with coordinating tax policies, and in evaluating the various hedging possibilities. Replacing manual operations is the simplest use of the computer, since no probability input is involved, and it appears cost-effective; many companies have now adopted similar EDP programs.

Simple Simulation Models

After development of an adequate data base, the use of simulation models allows the company to make assumptions, the classic 'what if' case, about future exchange rates and apply these to its present or projected positions. The model can identify gains or losses from any input scenario, including those arising from existing forward contracts. Tax assumptions must be built in, so that the user has a readily identifiable pattern of the net effects of rate changes on the company's structure. Sub-programs can evaluate best possibilities under different assumptions of interest and spot rate movements.

Such simple simulation models cannot predict future events, but provide an inexpensive way to test the effect on profits, taxes or liquidity of any potential rate changes. In thus helping the treasurer better to determine potential impact, hedging strategy is facilitated.

The absolute accuracy of future predictions is not mandatory and such models can quickly and inexpensively be run many times with different assumptions.

For example, the author was involved in an extended test to determine whether future spot rates could be predicted in a sufficiently narrow range to allow uncovered interest arbitrage to be undertaken at a profit consonant with the added risks involved. Uncovered arbitrage is essentially a spot purchase of currency B by an entity possessing and reporting in currency A, placing currency B on time deposit and reconverting to A at the end of the transaction.

A simple computer program using Monte Carlo techniques was designed to compare the probable yield of an unhedged investment in a number of alternative currencies. (Monte Carlo simulation involves the drawing of random numbers according to probability input by means of a random-number generator in order to test the distribution of results for a large number of likely circumstances. Since the randomness of expected exchange rates in the future is very great, this method allows many conceivable patterns to be tested and ranked.)

In the test a number of trading sources were asked to depict their predictions of future spot rates of various currencies at 2, 4 and 8 weeks forward in histogram form. Known information was the spot and deposit rates obtaining on the day of the investment for each alternative currency. Based on this data, the program processed in turn every alternative investment and so simulated the probable risks and potential yields of each alternative course of action.

The aim of the output was to give the decision-maker a ranking for each of the currencies available for investment, showing each alternative according to the rates of return or final yields that they could be expected to earn. The program was developed to assist in the following problem.

The treasurer of a German company could have DM1,000,000 which are not needed for 2 weeks. At the end of that time, however, Deutsche marks, and not any other currency, are required. A 2-week time deposit of these funds placed with a local German bank would yield 5% per annum at no risk. Alternatively, the treasurer could sell the Deutsche marks spot for sterling and obtain 8% per annum for a 2-week sterling deposit, while simultaneously contracting to sell the sterling forward for 2 weeks. At the maturity a fixed amount of Deutsche marks would be obtained, but the cost of forward cover will tend to cancel out the 3% interest differential in the rates of the two alternative currencies during the 2 weeks. Therefore, in limiting the capital risk, the potential return is reduced through the workings of the international interest arbitrage market back to approximately 5%.

The potential yield of such an investment made in a foreign currency may be substantially increased by carrying the investment on an unhedged basis, i.e. by waiting until the maturity of the sterling deposits before buying back Deutsche marks rather than buying them forward at the outset.

The final yield of such an unhedged investment will be dependent upon three variables: first, the exchange rate R1, at which marks can be sold for sterling on the day the investment is made; second, the interest rate that the 14-day sterling deposit could earn; and finally, the exchange rate, R2, at which the pounds could be sold and marks recovered on day 14, 2 weeks later. Two of these three variables are known at the time the decision to invest in sterling is taken: the exchange rate R1 and the sterling interest rate.

When traders were asked to predict R2 in histogram form in Bretton Woods days, their input was provided within a narrow range, as indeed spot rates were, and the accuracy was such that appreciable gains in uncovered transactions, compared to covered arbitrage, were obtainable. With the advent of floating rates, the forecasters were first unwilling and later unable to make histogram predictions which consistently allowed the same outcome, i.e. net appreciation from uncovered arbitrage. The range of histogram predictions encompassing all outcomes became very large, therefore of little use. As political factors began more and more to influence the markets, the ability to predict the magnitude, timing and direction of change fell off sharply. While a bank could still use the model to place funds, under the option to change its position almost instantaneously, the parameters of uncertainty were too great to allow corporations to make a similar decision, which for them is necessarily more static.

The table in Figure 19 is a sample of the output that was generated. The Deutsche mark investment is used as an example but with three alternative currencies for possible investments (French francs, Swiss francs and pound sterling), rather than sterling only.

Each column of the table compares the alternatives of keeping Deutsche marks in a German investment for 14 days earning an annual rate of 5%, with that obtained by investment in deposits in any of the three designated currencies (French francs, Swiss francs and sterling).

Figure 19. Output of Monte Carlo arbitrage model

	% chance to earn at least yield shown						
	20%	40%	50%	60%	70%	80%	90%
Yield for	FF(16%)	FF(12%)	SF(9%)	SF(7.8%)	SF(6.9%)	SF(6.5%)	SF(6%)
currency	£(13%)	£(11%)	FF(8%)	FF(7.4%)	£(6.7%)	£(6.2%)	£(5.8%)
shown	SF(12%)	SF(10%)	£(7.6%)	£(7.2%)	FF(6.6%)	FF(5.8%)	FF(5%)

(DM deposit would earn 5% for 14 days)

The 70% column, for example, shows that, based on the exchange rate predictions made, there is a 70% chance of obtaining a yield of 6.9% or higher if the decision is taken to invest in Swiss francs rather than Deutsche marks, and so on.

Mathematical Analysis

Advanced efforts attempt to simulate a multinational company's exchange risks and to formulate an optimal strategy to hedge them. Simulation may result in predicting models, used to forecast rate changes in the future, or decision-making models. In the latter, the framework is one of carefully modelling the firm and maximizing one function within assumptions of uncertainty, or selecting between alternatives.

The choice of technique in this field lies between optimization or heuristic models. Optimization models are normally restricted to one pre-determined objective: maximizing total profit or net worth functions normally, or minimizing costs, such as foreign exchange losses or conversion expense. An array of variables is analysed. After input of future probable rates, the model selects the best combination of variables to maximize or minimize an internally set goal, subject to any number of prescribed restrictions.

Heuristic models may be more useful for management decision-making in that they lay out the decision-making process, simulating as closely as possible the manner in which decisions would actually be taken by management in each set of circumstances. They make it possible to develop a hierarchy of objectives, allowing management to decide on the actual value of each objective or trade-off in the company's strategy.[1] These are essentially an expansion of the simple simulation models used to determine the impact of rate changes.

Further variations in mathematical applications are found in the distinction between stochastic or deterministic models. Stochastic models input the whole range of uncertainty and project the results for a wide range of future conditions. Deterministic models utilize only one set of given conditions, but can be run under various assumptions, allowing sensitivity analysis of any expected rate change.

Various companies, individuals or universities have tried to build full-scale models of one or more of these types. The modelling of the firm's structure is relatively straightforward. The greatest problems so far have been in the uncertainty aspects in the movement of future spot (and interest) rates. If the premise is accepted that economic factors do not now permit useful prediction of rates, then any short-term estimated range of future rates must of necessity be very broad. It is the author's opinion that projection of short- to medium-term exchange rate movements is now so uncertain as to be virtually useless and that single-point or narrow-band rate predictions are spurious.

For example, a major European company, among others, recently attempted to model its very complex trading and financial structure, adding projections of future exchange and interest rates in the countries in which it operates, and to optimize by linear programming the entire deployment of working capital. Its maximization goal was net profit after taxes; components of that profit were to come from interest yields, exchange appreciation and tax minimization. This called for analysis of all likely combinations of future exchange and interest rates: it became readily apparent that (i) future exchange rates could not be limited to a range narrow enough to let the program run without excessive and costly repetition, and (ii) the covariances between exchange markets and credit markets were not well enough known. For example, if the French franc depreciates, there will be some effect on the local Belgian franc borrowing rate. Statistical analysis has appeared ineffective in evaluating these covariance relationships and the problem becomes astronomical when dealing in two dozen or more exchange rates and credit markets.

Given this degree of uncertainty (which emphasizes the inability of quantitative methods to capture qualitative phenomena and shows that the whole international finance system needs more study), existing computer models are relatively inadequate. The company in question had a great deal of flexibility in its ability to change prices, currency of billing, to make short-term investments off-shore, to reverse, delay or accelerate funds flows. It was found that its major investment in modelling, however, could not be used cost-effectively, and it eventually scrapped the program.

The reader is referred to the Bibliography for a number of references in which present theory and attempts can be reviewed.

Rate Forecasting Techniques

A growing body of literature is concerned with the use of econometric computer models to forecast rates.[2] Essentially, such models use basic economic data, correlations and criteria for their analysis, as do economists. A wider range of variables can be input and the informational content of each type of variable can be both postulated and statistically tested after the fact.

Most models take the balance of payments position of a given country as the underlying predictive element in the determination of future spot exchange rates. The balance of payments itself, of course, is determined by a number of macro-economic, micro-economic and political forces. Model building thus concentrates on the relative movements of productivity and prices in each country. From the correlations thus ascertained, weighted by trade flows with each of the other countries, a range of balance of payments trends and theoretically the resultant parity changes can be extrapolated.

Some models use a very large number of variables, most of which themselves must be estimated or predicted on the basis of historical data. Given uncertainty and the relative lack of correlation between these variables, the actual accuracy of such rate forecasting has not yet proven to be within a range acceptably narrow for the corporate treasurer. While proponents of such models claim that speculative activity does not usually run counter to the basic strength of a currency, many observers would argue that speculative movements of funds are both critical and unpredictable and that they make short-term spot rate predictions untenable.[3] Only in the longer term do computer models offer any guidance, showing the sensitivity of various optimization programmes to rate changes, not yet in rate prediction itself.

Notes

1. See Folks, William R. Jr. 'Decision analysis for exchange risk management', *Financial Management*, Winter 1972, for an excellent example of this approach, using expected utility as its focus.
2. Among others:
   Gaillot, Henry J., 'Purchasing power parity as an explanation of long term changes in exchange rates' *Journal of Money, Credit and Banking*, 2, No. 3, August 1970.
   Shulman, R. B., 'Are foreign exchange risks measurable?' *Columbia Journal of World Business*, May—June 1970.
3. This is well argued in Dufey, Gunter and Giddy, Ian H. 'Forecasting exchange rates in a floating world', *Euromoney*, November 1975.

CHAPTER 12

Integration with Liquidity Management

The emphasis in this text on the foreign exchange risks of the corporation should not cloud the fact that these are directly related to all facets of liquidity management. The two management areas are interrelated and inseparable parts of the same process, dealing with an uncertain and restricted external world. This chapter briefly depicts the role of liquidity management in the firm and the need to integrate closely both functions, which are very similar in structure and intent.

Liquidity management is concerned with controlling, investing and preserving the monetary assets of the firm, and with structuring a rational investment or borrowing policy. In a one-country setting, this control function is one of identifying cash surpluses and cash needs at the various domestic locations during the production/sales cycle on a present and forecast basis. Here, the chief problem is one of identifying cash needs and sources in advance, so that appropriate funding or borrowing procedures can be undertaken, and of eliminating the chances that funds will be unutilized somewhere in the system. Given a single tax and legal system and no currency risk, this primarily relies on good portfolio management, banking relationships and cash forecasting.

Liquidity held or borrowed in the international firm is affected by each of the many factors already discussed.[1] Its disposition is controlled and limited by exchange control barriers, which usually prohibit the flow of funds in the most favourable directions. Funds held by individual subsidiaries in different countries cannot be considered fungible and there is little or no chance of wide-scale pooling of funds. Even intracountry liquidity management can be affected by tax laws and weak capital markets which offer few investment media or banking systems which delay transfers. Expropriation or funds blockage is a continual possibility in certain parts of the world.

Above all, international liquidity management cannot be divorced from exchange factors. Almost every borrowing/investment decision made is implicitly an exchange-related one. To leave funds in one country, to convert and deposit them covered or uncovered, or to lend them internationally, involves an acceptance or a transmittal of exchange risks. Uncertainty about future rates shapes or obfuscates the policy of the international treasurer in liquidity decisions as it does in his attempt to optimize exchange management.

Liquidity management directly embodies the fragmentation which characterizes the multinational firm. Government monetary or financial policies, specifically those designed to influence the balance of payments, can limit the deployment of the firm's working capital. Most government measures over the last 10 years, although constructed on macro-economic grounds, can be seen as hampering the international company's micro-economic liquidity policies. The OFDI sharply limited the ability to lend U.S. parent liquidity abroad and constrained the balances permitted in certain (chiefly European) areas. The German Bardepot directly limited liquidity influx into Germany by making external loans and leading/lagging measures subject to a confiscatory reserve. The Japanese approached the problem by insisting on letter-of-credit transactions and/or formal approval for many types of credit/financing facilities. Most long-established exchange control systems in the West — the U.K., France, Belgium and Italy for example — have an array of measures designed to filter (or prohibit) the effects of liquidity movements upon their domestic economies. Most exchange controls are geared either towards blocking funds outflow or to discouraging funds inflow for monetary policy reasons. Sometimes a single country may establish exchange control mechanisms of both types concurrently, which makes the task of liquidity management extremely complicated.

Given these parameters, the discipline of international liquidity management is precisely akin to that used in exchange management; this similarity can significantly assist the integration of the two areas. Liquidity management must also be centrally coordinated and directed by a control point which has full knowledge of resources and needs. Normally, this function will be based at the parent level, although it may be partially delegated to regional centres. Local implementation of policy may be carried out with appropriate autonomy.

Liquidity management, like exchange management, needs to be based on a detailed, treasury-oriented reporting system which goes beyond that necessary for accounting purposes. It must be anticipatory, fostering proper determination of liquidity implications of all financial transactions in advance. It should allow a proper response by forecasting liquidity shortages or uninvested surpluses.

It can readily be seen that the reporting system used for foreign exchange policy will include virtually all necessary elements for the review of liquidity decisions. In fact, liquidity/cash budgeting is an integral part of the exchange management reporting mechanism.

The implications of centralization on profit centre accounting are also similar. If it is accepted that foreign exchange gains/losses should be eliminated from the internal operating reports of subsidiaries, so might be interest income/costs beyond purely local levels (i.e. where directed from above). This correction eliminates both types of financial adjustments from internal operating statements without eliminating local responsibility to keep asset levels down.

Centralization can assist in reducing the total amount of liquidity needed by the corporation, and therefore its exchange risk. Total assets held abroad and their related financing costs may be minimized. The specialized knowledge to place and optimize the use of liquidity can more easily be built up in one central location, and has ready access to tax and accounting assistance which the local locations may not enjoy. As in the foreign exchange management area, only a central point is in a position to see all liquidity shortfalls and surpluses, to appraise different market rates and evaluate interest arbitrage opportunities.

Furthermore, the advantages of centralization necessary for exchange decisions are bolstered by centralizing the liquidity decision, if not necessarily its local deployment. Perhaps the greatest impetus towards, and foundation for, close integration of the two fields of liquidity and exposure is the need to examine any financial decision from both aspects. Two examples reiterate this point, already implied earlier. A Canadian affiliate of a U.S. group has surplus funds for 3 months. It can leave them in local currency time deposits at 7% per annum with commercial banks, place them in U.S. dollars at 6%, or in pounds sterling at 9%. Even assuming that the creditworthiness of the deposit institutions or commercial paper issuers is equal, the liquidity management decision cannot be looked at from the interest yield aspect alone. The highest yield, not surprisingly is found in a potentially weaker currency. On the other hand, there is a probability that no change, or even a positive one, between the Canadian dollar or the pound might occur, and the maximum yield for the group might be obtained by investing in sterling deposits. Even if the subsidiary takes the most conservative course of leaving funds in local time deposits, this has an exchange implication for the group as well. Since the Canadian subsidiary cannot know the other Canadian dollar or pound commitments of the group, nor its future overall cash needs and investment plans, it should accept central guidance, at least in coordination of such decisions.

Assuming the Canadian subsidiary could also lend those same funds to a subsidiary in another country, the liquidity management decision once again must take into account not only the appropriate yield/cost which each partner would face in lending/borrowing from third parties, but also the exchange risk for one (or both) parties in the transaction.

Liquidity management encounters much the same uncertainty and unpredictable environment as does exposure risk analysis. It is not surprising that mathematical techniques and computer applications are avidly sought here as well. As a generalization, those programs which seek to isolate liquidity optimization techniques under uncertainty appear to be more useful than the linear programming techniques concerning exchange gain optimization, perhaps because the former area is an offshoot of the older, well-developed field of portfolio management.

The corporation's attitude to risk enters again when the two fields are treated as one. The placing of international liquidity is a function of the yield curve of the tenor and of risk of the investment medium or currency. If the instrument is in a currency other than that of the holder, or of the holder's natural inflows, an added level of risk is present. In the Canadian case above, the decision to take or reject a 9% yield in sterling would depend largely on the corporation's risk profile and assessment of the Canadian dollar/pound cross-rates over 3 months. Since these functions vary by company, there is no specific 'right' answer.

A number of generic ways in which liquidity can be utilized internationally can be depicted:

1. Parallel loans with companies in a second country, in which each side makes its local currency available to a subsidiary of the other for a fixed period of time;
2. Covered arbitrage abroad;
3. Uncovered arbitrage abroad;
4. Extending longer credit to importing affiliates;
5. Pre-paying import payables: to affiliates,
   to third parties;
6. Intercompany lending to foreign affiliates.

(There are others; of course, not every country allows all of these types of action.)

All of these can also be looked upon as hedging tactics. No uncovered liquidity movement will have a neutral effect on exposure by definition (except the first in a limited sense) and it is a moot point whether the corporate treasurer, grappling with an array of assets and risks, should turn first to the liquidity problem or the exchange risk aspects. Since the risk of parity change is the common denominator, assessment of that risk first should be the initiative to analysing all opportunities.

The use of vehicle companies applies to both areas equally. If a major use of the intermediary reinvoicing or confirming vehicle is to centralize exposure and exposure strategy in an off-shore low tax area, the same advantages accrue in liquidity deployment. International funds are taken out of the limits of local exchange control restrictions and put into the hands of a vehicle where few or no liquidity and exchange restrictions exist. Such centralization of funds is as close to international pooling as is now possible; by using the network of intercompany trade and other transactions in a sophisticated manner, adjustment of credit terms can change, augment or draw-down liquidity as desired. A vehicle company creates more ties between the subsidiaries, even where there is no direct trade between them, and materially increases the flexibility and range of management action as it does for exchange management. The network of intercompany linkages thereby created is among the more powerful tools open to the large, sophisticated company which has the initiative to create, and the understanding to operate successfully, such a company.

Finally, liquidity management is affected by mechanical impediments in the exchange/banking/mail systems. An appreciable portion of a company's apparent liquidity may in fact be delayed or in transit due to the slowness of customers in paying and of banks in transferring funds in settlement of international transactions. These inefficiencies and delays may diminish liquidity, impair credit management and add to the general difficulties of financial management.

They can often be circumvented by funds interception or acceleration techniques, ideally with a high degree of automaticity. These in turn are based on selecting the best payment routes, making customer instructions more precise and cutting out administrative and processing stages. When implemented, the acceleration and better identification of cash inflows can materially help liquidity management.

Liquidity and exchange management can be seen as the two chief facets of International Money Management. Based on the same constraints and uncertainties, sharing common goals of income maximization and protection of assets, they should be jointly approached. Integrated with each other, the two concerns should likewise be coordinated with tax policy to form an optimal International Money Management system that will incorporate cash management techniques and build a structured approach on that foundation to control the global assets of the company, whether this involves their deployment, funding or protection against risk.

Note
1. For an outstanding portrayal of the field see Goeltz, Richard K., 'Managing liquid funds on an international scale', Presentation made to American Management Association Conference on International Cash Management, New York, November 1971. He is treasurer of Seagrams.

CHAPTER 13

Integration with Tax Strategy

That foreign exchange management needs to be integrated at all times with tax strategy is explicit throughout this study. Every foreign exchange decision and every realized transaction will have a tax implication to be considered. The tax element in international business, in fact, is possibly more essential than that of foreign exchange per se, since correct tax strategy decisions can outweigh the total foreign exchange risks of the average company. The logic of this statement can be seen in several ways:

(1) The international firm can virtually eliminate transaction exposure by invoicing and borrowing only in each affiliate's currency and covering foreign currency commitments to third parties, such as for imports, forward. Many translation exposures can similarly be covered. Tax assessments are a continual and unavoidable condition of doing business abroad.

(2) Foreign exchange risks fall into only certain asset/liability categories and income elements; taxes range across the whole gamut of transactions undertaken.

(3) Foreign exchange cover costs are in a limited range of, say, 2—5% per annum; even the projected range of potential spot rate changes in a given reporting period is unlikely to exceed 15—20%. Corporate tax rate *differentials*, since these are the critical factors, range up to 50%. (Differential rates can arise either in the differences between the average corporate tax rates in different countries, or in a situation where one subsidiary pays a 50% rate and another, with a loss carry forward position, pays effectively 0%.) The loss of tax credits which could be used to reduce corporate taxes on income by poor planning can also be material.

(4) Foreign exchange parities are a function of individual countries' monetary policy, but tend to be a passive component. The usual attitude of government is to protect an exchange rate against inflows/ outflows arising from a fundamental disequilibrium or to let it slowly adjust to market forces in order not to become a destabilizing force. Tax policy is a much more active tool, used directly and frequently by government as an instrument of economic policy, and subject to large, sometimes politically based, changes.

The conclusion from the above is not to downgrade exchange risk management, but to stress its proper integration with the overall financial strategy of the company and particularly with tax planning. The analysis going into a proper coordination of exchange risk strategy will take into account fiscal elements as a prime consideration. The tactical side will also consider the tax effect, or lack thereof, on each type of exchange-oriented transaction: forward contracts, inter-company loans, dividend payments, etc.

To analyse all the tax considerations in international business requires several full-length books, which can be found elsewhere.[1] This chapter describes instead the nature of tax strategy and the manner in which tax analysis should be brought into exposure management. It also gives a summary review of the present characteristic tax treatments applying to the basic types of accounting and transaction risks found in international dealings.

The Nature of Tax Strategy

No precise treatment of tax strategy has yet been agreed upon, since a variety of attitudes towards taxes exists in international companies. A common policy is to minimize total taxes to the greatest extent possible, another to delay their payment similarly. The most rational approach would appear to be that expounded by Chown in his excellent survey *Taxation and Multinational Enterprise*,[2] in which he promulgates the maximization of post-tax income worldwide. The total amount of taxes paid is subordinate to the net income engendered in the various areas of operation and to the incremental value of direct income generated by tax planning.

The methodology of tax planning, no matter what end goal is decided upon, is much like that described in the preceding chapters. Tax planning is concerned with the impact of a complex outside environment in the financial performance of the company, specifically with the effect of tax assessments on profit potential. Like exchange management, it is anticipatory and based on a perception of future positions, risks or obligations. The tax input is critical in project planning, where the viability, location, method and potential partners in the project have an influence on the ultimate decision and form. All financing decisions need to have tax input; most International Money Management techniques can change radically the tax vulnerability of the group if this is not understood.

The nature of tax planning is, therefore, consonant with foreign exchange exposure strategy. Both require expanded reporting/communications systems and a centralized approach. Tax strategy needs to have precise information on the regulatory and market framework of each individual transaction envisioned and its ultimate effect. The need to understand the existence and guidelines of double taxation treaties, for example, mirrors the need of the international treasurer to understand exchange control and regulatory barriers to fund movements or hedging. Since tax systems differ as widely as exchange control regulations, the ability to change the source of income arising under different tax structures parallels the desire to be able to shift exchange gains or losses to other locations. Both policies coalesce at this point.

The Tax Framework in Foreign Exchange

The underlying principle of taxation in the foreign exchange area lies in the concept of realized transactions. With few exceptions, fiscal authorities will tax only completed transactions, i.e. forward contracts at maturity or actual conversions. The accounting treatment of exchange gains/losses is complementary in that accounting conventions now prescribe (or lean toward) the two-transaction approach: an export credit sale in foreign currency is broken into the actual sales price in local value and a separate foreign exchange transaction involving a future receipt of currency. The gain or loss on the second half of the operation is treated separately. In the cash transactions of a company, therefore, the two approaches have a common philosophy.

In the consolidation area, however, tax and accounting orientations diverge sharply. As shown in Chapter 2, the translation of foreign accounts into a common base currency will create 'losses' or 'gains' for the parent of a multinational group, which are publicly reported in many countries. These accounting results have no direct tax effects, (although realization of those positions in the future will be taxable). A reported loss on translation of long-term debt denominated in Swiss francs will not reduce the taxes of the parent company in the U.K. or the U.S. The 'loss' is reported for bookkeeping purposes but tells little about the economic position of the firm. A loss in one period can be reversed at a later date. For this reason, tax authorities usually neither tax unrealized gains, nor allow credits against actual taxes for unrealized losses, thereby coming closer to the concept of economic risk than do many accounting principles.

Given the importance of tax considerations in the overall management of the firm, the distinction between completed and unrealized transactions underpins the emphasis in this text on covering that economic exposure, rather than only translation exposure. Defined as the after-tax and after-rate change effect of completed transactions, the goal of economic exposure management is precisely that of tax management, i.e. the maximization of realized earnings. This should be seen as complementary to the considerations underlying accounting presentation of results; the different ways in which individual firms might look at either result have already been outlined.

The dichotomy of taxable and non-taxable effects on apparently straightforward transactions has to be analysed in all exchange matters and is particularly important in the hedging decision. The standard ways in which each cross-border activity is usually taxed are reviewed below.

Tax Treatment of Exchange Transactions
1. Realized Trade and Financial Transactions

Under the completed transactions rule, unaffected by whether company accountants have in fact divided a transaction into its original sales portion and a future settlement portion, fiscal authorities will probably look at the completed sale as one element of income and the later settlement as a second element. Losses before settlement on receivables/payables have no taxable effect until realized and are not unlike losses arising from a domestic credit sale where full repayment was not achieved. The actual gain or loss under the two-transaction theory will be calculated from the difference between the booked sales price and the equivalent in local currency received from the settlement in foreign exchange. These transactions, and the hedges usually associated with them, will fall into normal ordinary income.

Other types of transaction, longer-term in nature, can give rise to the same dichotomization in tax effect. A British company may make a U.S. direct investment and finance this with a U.S. dollar loan. If, over time, the pound depreciates and the investment is ultimately sold, the gain on disposal is taxable. This gain in sterling terms may be entirely due to the movement of currencies. However, the loss on the loan repayment is not presently tax-deductible.

2. Hedging Transactions

The asymmetry of tax effects on some hedging transactions was already mentioned in Chapter 8. Where a forward contract has covered an outstanding receivable or payable, both are completed at maturity and both fall into ordinary income treatment. Where a forward contract is taken out to cover a translation risk, gains on the former are taxable at maturity but not losses on the latter. Normally, gains on exchange contracts will be taxable at full corporate rates, or around 50% for profitable concerns in Western Europe and North America. This necessitates grossing-up of the cover unless it is taken by a tax-free vehicle.

Gains on forward contracts can fall under lower capital gains rates in certain cases, primarily when they have been held more than 6 months and are sold before maturity. The normal rule here depends on the length and uncompleted nature of the contract. If the contract is closed, i.e. held until the maturity date, the gain or loss on it will probably be of an ordinary nature and taxed accordingly. Foreign currency will be deemed to have passed hands and the corporate principal will have held the currency less than 6 months.

However, a long-term forward contract can be considered a capital asset, and under the conditions listed above, its pre-maturity sale can result in long-term capital gains (losses) with resultant tax amelioration. The sale of the contract has to be absolute, with the new holder taking over the remaining exchange risk.

The Internal Revenue Service in the U.S. has in two cases — *Corn Products*[3] and *International Flavors and Fragrances*[4] — designated a hedging contract as having engendered ordinary income. The crux of this dispute is whether forward contracts are in fact integral and usual components of a company's international business. At the time of writing, the issue is still unresolved in the U.S. and no clear definition of which transactions fall under capital gains treatment can be given. Tax counsel's advice should be sought in any specific actual case.

3. Intercompany Transactions

The assumption is still made that intercompany transactions have no impact on a company's consolidated exchange exposure. In the event of rate movements, the pre-tax gain of one side would be exactly equivalent to the pre-tax loss of the other side in terms of the parent currency. The impact on the company as a whole would then be a function of the difference between tax rates in each country. As long as both companies are profitable and located in Western industrial countries this would be a matter of only a few percentage points in the gross gain or loss calculation.

Numerous examples in the text have shown that this is often a misleading assumption. The tax differentials between subsidiaries may vary widely. Furthermore, the nature of the transaction itself is important. Outstanding intercompany positions at the time of a rate change will in fact be offset to an extent by the different effects on both parties. But these commitments can be changed before rate movements to minimize the negative impact, or established exactly to put the company in a certain position.

The tax effects of this must be integrated by the treasurer with other input in preparing the overall hedging strategy and carrying out its specific implementation. Where possible, the use of different locations to bear the tax on profitable exchange contracts for hedging purposes parallels attempts to optimize other financial transactions which involve exchange considerations.

Attitude of Tax Authorities Towards Multinational Transactions

A note about the increasing awareness of customs and tax authorities of the practices of multinational companies is in order. Given the enormous publicity about such companies in recent years and the sometimes misdirected attacks of Congressional or world organization committees upon them, the public knowledge of all types of multinational transactions has also sharpened the scrutiny which regulatory bodies apply to cross-border flows. Intercompany transactions arouse particular attention, both about their underlying price and the currency rate used for billing. Divergences in either area can result in demands for explanation and/or tax audits. The use of transfer pricing is increasingly questionable, and currency rates used for booking intercompany transactions should be kept at arm's length, as shown on p. 65.

Notes

1. Among others, Ravencroft, Donald R., *Taxation and Foreign Currency*, Cambridge: Harvard University Law School, 1973 and Frommel, S. N., *Taxation of Branches and Subsidiaries in Western Europe, Canada and the U.S.A.*, London: Kluwer-Harrap, 1975.
2. Chown, John F., *Taxation and Multinational Enterprise*, London: Longman, 1974.
3. Corn Products Refining Co. vs Commissioner, 350 US 46 (1955).
4. International Flavors and Fragrances Inc. vs Commissioner, 62 T.C. 232 (1974), on appeal to 2nd Circuit (C.A.-2).

CHAPTER 14

Personnel Implications of Centralizing Exposure Management

A major theme in this volume has been the need to centralize exchange exposure management and to base it upon the widest possible internal and external information. Its mode of action was seen to be anticipatory and directive. By necessity, only one central point can determine and assess all the company's risks and hedging alternatives. This centralization, however, can have negative implications for foreign personnel and for management evaluation systems. It is important to recognize and overcome these, since the input of local finance/accounting personnel abroad, as well as the understanding of general management and marketing staff of the nature of exchange risk, is essential. As risk management is the subject of this volume, an inferred risk here would be that local personnel, seeing their role diminished, will not support the effort sufficiently. Both the underlying information and the development of policy could suffer.

Local Resistance to Centralization

Centralization of the financial management function can have a severe effect on, and will be resisted by, local management. Given that exchange risk strategy setting and liquidity management could be listed as among the most interesting financial activities, taking away of local responsibilities in this field may seriously diminish the motivation of foreign managers. General managers may also take an interest and be personally involved in exchange management; their reaction will be similar.

Furthermore, the income of local managers is often geared to profit levels and profit increases. The result of shifting of exchange gains and particularly of interest income will be seen not only as immediately cutting down the profits reported internally to senior management, but also as having an unfavourable effect on salary or bonuses. The best finance managers abroad may also see centralization as a denigration of their own abilities, a repudiation of their local input or as a loss of training and broadening of experience.

In these suppositions, real or imagined, there lies a significant danger to coordination of strategy and tactics. The input, motivation and training of local personnel continue to be as critical as before in providing the total information input. Their local knowledge and contact with local markets and institutions is broadly supportive of, and probably indispensable to, the whole financial management effort. No finance executive can pontificate in the Mid-West, the Midlands or the Ruhr and direct exposure tactics by fiat. If total knowledge of risks and alternatives is conceptually the core of exposure management, local input — of data, projections and market constraints — is the base of its structure. The integration of local knowledge and the continued motivation of local officials are therefore essential. To a large extent, these can be assured by correct intercompany reporting and proper setting of responsibilities, coupled with interchange of visits and personnel. This means that the firm should not only augment reporting systems which depict corporate financial positions, but should also review internal management control systems which evaluate local performance.

Management Evaluation Systems

The internal reports used for management evaluation differ from those presented to the tax authorities or to stockholders. In very general terms, local subsidiaries are evaluated on the basis of return on investment, return on or reduction of working capital, profits as a proportion of sales, or similar formulae. In standard management control systems, net profit is compared to a specified denominator (assets, sales, capital, etc.). This normally includes interest income/ exposure and exchange gains/losses in the calculation of income.

A measure to adapt any such standard system to one where a control point takes responsibility for such gains and losses is to remove them from the evaluation of subsidiary performance, including all or the directed portion of interest exposure/income. (In the latter event, interest expense incurred to finance local working capital, specifically inventory and receivables, remains so that these stay under control, but that arising from local borrowings for hedging purposes or inter-company loans is eliminated.) The bottom line then becomes operating profits less financial charges, which is likely to be a better measure of local operating performance in any case.

In many recent cases, local management (or the divisional management at parent level) have been quite willing to give away responsibility for exchange gains or losses, since in unpredictable markets losses are at least as likely as gains. In certain liquid companies, there has been more resistance to elimination of interest income even if the local investment thereof is not optimal on a group basis. The adoption of revised management evaluation systems has not been a substantial point of contention, since in an important way these act against the main impediments to the acceptance of centralization.

Difficulties of Evaluating Performance of Foreign Subsidiaries

A management problem which often arises in this regard is the analysis of local subsidiary results when these are obscured by translation into the parent currency. Head Office executives, when looking at actual performance versus budget, will tend to do this in terms of their own currency of reference. They may compare current results with those of preceding years in parent currency terms without evaluating the operational aspects of judging results accomplished in two periods of different rates. For example, a 10% rise in sales with a 15% rise in profits, both in local currency terms, could be under-estimated if a significant depreciation of local currency had occurred against the currency in which top management reviews that performance. For this reason, many multinationals have correctly moved to analysis of local currency statements to compare period by period results and performance.

The Finance Department as a Profit Centre

Management evaluation systems which internally reapportion exchange adjustments and interest factors to the finance department/ treasury allow it to be designated as a profit centre, recording its own revenues and expenditures. Correct internal systems will be able to identify those local gains and losses which have resulted from central decisions and those changes in interest earned or interest paid which arise from leading/lagging or loans directed to change various entities' exposure or liquidity.

These effects should have no validity in evaluation of local performance and should be accounted for and imputed to the financial profit centre. In a wider sense, the group translation losses/gains and related hedging expenses would be apportioned similarly.

In this manner, the performance of the finance department itself can be better evaluated, since there are not other accounting mechanisms which do so. It seems inconsistent to give responsibility for exchange risk and treasury management to a staff function without the ability to ascertain the costs, in terms of additional staff and information as well as financial expenses, and benefits of doing so. Correctly constituted, the move to a profit centre could foster better understanding of the treasury function. For U.S. companies, the elimination of accounting reserves will make the establishment of such control systems more difficult. The inability to record all financial factors involved in the decision-making process, such as the cash flow effect of borrowing at a lower interest cost where reduced interest expense is not quantified but later exchange losses from appreciation of borrowings are, should be met by discussions and reviews with top management which go beyond statistical reports.

Redetermining Local Responsibilities

Revamping of internal evaluation systems does not solve the human problems of centralization and the resultant direct intervention from headquarters. The company imposing a central control system of financial management falls under the geocentric or manipulative structural alternatives now under intense analysis by a number of academic disciplines.[1] In both types of firms, the critical factors remain:

1. If exchange gains/losses and factors items are taken from the control of local management, how can their support be assured?
2. Will they then ignore the exchange risk area or their commitment to provide qualitative as well as quantitative data to the central office?
3. If interest expense is eliminated, will their control over inventory or accounts receivable deteriorate?

A first step in resolving these potential problems is to state clearly the operating responsibilities of each local manager. These functions can be spelled out in such a way that local officials are convinced of the importance of their role. A well-developed personnel policy here would have important morale effects.

1. Carrying Out Hedging Transactions Locally

The decision to cover or accept risk will be made centrally, but the actual hedging actions to reduce or cover transaction risk are substantially carried out at local levels. Documentation is prepared in the field. The finance managers of local companies have responsibility to negotiate with local banks and obtain rate offers for hedging; they will sometimes have discretion as to timing or the local covering decision. This complements the usual need to deal locally for transactions involving countries with exchange control. Of course, the financial control centre may independently obtain rate quotes before large local transactions are carried out.

2. Providing Reporting Input

The accuracy and timeliness of data supplied to management remain the responsibility of the local staff. This task is more challenging and should be more interesting to the local manager in the area of forecast data. The whole process of budgeting sales, working capital items, etc., by amount and then by currency rests directly on the subsidiary's financial staff; the better of these will see this process as part of the educational experience they desire.

3. Maintaining Contact with Local Officials

Hedging and compliance with local regulations involve close rapport with local bankers and local government officials. Clear direction for foreign managers to keep abreast of market and administrative developments not only adds to total information/forecasting flows, but also to motivation. These contacts are important in both strategy and its implementation. The multinational firm needs to be represented by capable officials abroad, having close rapport with outside financial and government colleagues.

Government contacts should range over many areas, such as trade departments, taxation authorities and central banking and exchange control officials. The anticipatory side of financial management can be assisted if knowledge of the pressures on governments is understood, pressures which may lead to changes in regulations in any of these areas. In-depth understanding of the government's social and economic policies can best be gleaned locally; in carrying out tactical changes in exposure and liquidity positions, local knowledge of regulations and precedents is invaluable.

4. Supplying Data Bank Information

A functional part of local responsibility, if not always an invigorating one, is the updating of local regulatory and market changes. Intercompany sources of such information are more efficient and more directly usable than most outside agencies can be. It should be pointed out that this responsibility remains a major one.

The evaluation of subsidiary officials, therefore, shifts away from a directly visible one involving the reported profit and loss accounts to a supportive one in the supplying of data and contacts with local officials. While less challenging in some ways, it can be put forward as a sine qua non in the exchange management process.

A problem can occur where local managers report first to a local general manager, with only dotted-line reporting to parent or regional headquarters treasury staff. The local general manager may have his own reasons to ensure that figures are seen in the most favourable light. While this will not mean that accounting figures reported to headquarters are deliberately misleading, it can materially weaken the link between local finance expertise and central treasury needs. The finance official abroad, dependent on his own general manager for promotion and salary increases, may find it difficult to warn his head office about trends or future risks about which he is concerned and of which they should be informed. This could be particularly critical in those interpretive or anticipatory areas which statistical data do not make apparent.

To combat this problem, formal links between and responsibility from local finance to head office staff are essential. Some firms go so far as to require reviews of field personnel shifting or firing to be approved by Head Office.

Intercompany Contacts

A rewarding way to keep up the motivation and assure the input of local finance staff is to increase the contacts between international managers and to promote the exchange of personnel. Many companies make the mistake of directing all affairs from the centre, with only annual junkets by a senior financial officer to the major locations. Leaving aside the potential need for headquarters companies in many cases, its is suggested that the average company sharply increase its intercompany contacts, both through visits of affiliate finance managers to the home office and through international or regional finance meetings. The latter can be used to discuss accounting and International Money Management matters, including exchange exposure; cross-fertilization in the cases known to the author has far outweighed the overheads involved.

Bringing the group finance personnel together, if properly devised, can give them a picture of the risks, problems and strategies of the whole group. Their own role and that of each subsidiary are made vividly apparent; their input and support can more readily be solicited. Many surveys have reiterated the communication value in such face-to-face contact, the level and depth of which go far beyond written or telephone possibilities, and which also promotes the local motivation which is the concern of this chapter.[2]

Notes

1. See Rutenberg, David P., 'Organizational Archetypes of a Multinational Company', *Management Science*, February 1970, which gives a review of the main studies of personnel organization and communications in international firms.
2. This is, of course, a cursory review of a very complex area, not directly included in financial management. A wealth of literature already exists on the field, despite the relatively recent awareness that multinationals have new or different motivational problems from domestic firms.

   A standard text is Dalton, Gene W. and Lawrence, Paul R., *Motivation and Control in Organizations*, Homewood, Illinois; Irwin, 1971, which includes a useful bibliography. Experiences of many U.S. multinationals are summarized in National Industrial Conference Board *Managing the International Financial Function*, Studies in Business Policy No. 133, New York, 1970. See also Ginzberg, Eli and Reilley, Ewing W., *Effecting Change in Large Organizations*, New York: Columbia University Press, 1957.

CHAPTER 15

Summary

This volume has presented a coordinated and sequential approach to the area of foreign exchange management. It is predicated on a belief that economic stresses and imbalances will lead to continuing exchange market turbulence and rate movements, despite the best efforts of monetary authorities. The problems these fluctuating conditions create for international business fall into all spheres of financial management and bring a variety of risks.

It is the author's contention, that the resultant exchange exposure can be identified and controlled by a *centralized system*, itself based on sufficient information and detail to prepare a cohesive and anticipatory strategy. This data will chiefly already exist in the accounting records of the firm, although few examples can be found which automatically give the treasury department sufficient internal information for its response. Instead, the treasury must find ways directly to tap the company's records without waiting for balance sheet compilation and cash flow analysis to go through the usual accounting/controllership routing.

Exchange exposure management, above all, was seen to be *anticipatory*. This puts particular emphasis on forecasting systems, both of cash flows and projected balance sheet alterations. That necessity can require additional reporting elements, again not always of a type normally produced by the accounting mechanism.

If this centralized and anticipatory framework is adopted, then much of the approach to this complex area follows a step-by-step logic. At the outset, the department responsible for exposure management will need to define the various types of risk which exchange exposure implies for the particular firm. The accounting exposure risk consists of potential effects on published statements when currencies possessed or owed by any entity of the group and corresponding income streams are translated into a common base currency used by the parent company. Translation of consolidated income will follow certain prescribed local accounting conventions, as will consolidation of the group balance sheet. Many of the recorded exchange adjustments will have no immediate fiscal effect on the concern except for realized transactions of the parent. Although the reported results themselves may have unacceptable implications, the finance department should look equally at transactions, some of which are eliminated in accounting terms, but which present an actual operating risk to the group or any one entity. This *economic exposure* can arise in intercompany accounts or loans, in inventory and other items. It may also have material importance for future cash flows, profits or even direct investment. Definition of this area of exchange exposure requires 'looking beyond the balance sheet' and an analysis which is removed from the traditional concept of accounting risk.

Transactional exposures of this kind are among the more critical faced in exposure management, and a goal of the treasury department should be to eliminate these transactional risks where possible on a cost-effective basis. Whether translation gains and losses are completely eliminated is a function of the risk profile of the individual company, its industry rivals and the requirement, or lack thereof, to publish financial results. Economic or transaction exposures, on the other hand, may negatively affect the assets of the company, which it is the treasury's job to protect, conserve or increase.

This does not necessarily mean covering by forward contracts alone, which may be one of the last hedging possibilities considered. Forward deals are limited in any event by many regulatory authorities. Instead, there is a whole array of internal corporate and external market techniques available to the multinational firm to redirect or eliminate its exposures. Their selection, particularly those dealing with inter-company transactions, can mistakenly be based on intuition rather than a systematic cost analysis. The finance department should develop its information systems to allow an analysis of the cost/yield aspects of changing its exposed position by both internal and external methods.

The additional detail needed to understand all elements of exposure in the first place will permit a better appraisal of the ability to lead or lag payments, to change currencies of billing, to increase prices or to consider structural changes in the company itself. Market data and the creation of a data bank on regulatory and fiscal constraints should improve the choice of external methods used to complement internal adjustments. All hedging techniques have an explicit or implicit cost; it is the identification of these costs and the comparison of them with exposed risk positions and projected rate movements which is the beginning of a balanced management of risk.

Emphasis was placed in the text on an anticipatory approach to the field. The best data system imaginable is of little use when it contains no forecasts of future positions. Strategy based solely on a perception of present risk can be costly or misguided in a period of changing corporate positions. Forecasting of at least the direction and timing of such internal changes is critical. While this is always a difficult field, there are a number of mathematical tools, particularly ratio analysis, which can assist in the process.

An adequate reporting system will depict the present balance sheet position by currency of the group on a consolidated basis and that of each separate entity. It will attempt to do the same for selected future dates. Properly constituted, reports will show both the translation risks of the firm over the short to medium term and the transaction or economic risks of any part of the group. Income stream trends and the potential rate change effects will be determined for each operating currency by cash flow forecasts. Together with that array of exchange exposure and liquidity reports, external data on structural constraints will show the parameters on internal or external hedging possibilities.

To repeat a point made in the text, this detailed reporting is not as costly or laborious as it appears at first glance. Virtually all of that data is available somewhere in the company's records, most often in the perimeter of foreign subsidiaries, although forecasting will usually have to be strengthened. What is required is a redirecting to and reassimilation of that information in a central control point in the treasury.

Once this is accomplished, the determination of impact on any one firm becomes a process of matching future expected rate changes on the positions maintained and expected to be maintained by the group on a currency-by-currency basis. Determining that impact involves an assessment of market trends which can be put in terms of probability, although presently including a wide range of short-term expected rates. The unpredictability of the mid-1970s markets does not allow precise projections of rates within the rather short-term maturity range examined by the treasurer. Enough of a direction can be postulated, however, to make the after-tax impact of parity changes sufficiently apparent.

Creating a strategy to deal with that perception is a function of the individual firm's attitude to risk. A maximization of earnings policy might foster a different strategy from one which was directed towards preservation of assets or maintenance of sales volumes. If a firm's policy is simply to protect reported income, it might consider covering all risks, which would be appropriate for the simple exporting or importing firm.

The coverage of all possible exchange risks over time, however, has proved to be more expensive than covering on a selective basis. Instead, the more aggressive firm should decide which potential risks are unacceptable from the point of view of potential realized losses and effects on profits or liquidity of the firm. This will include bookkeeping or translation losses as well, if these are considered an important risk.

In theory, each firm would make a cost/risk analysis based on the above criteria, its own particular risk structure and flexibility in hedging its risks. The logic in covering only certain of those would derive from the calculation of individual risks in each currency, deciding which are acceptable and which are unacceptable, and selecting one or an array of methods to cover the latter at the lowest cost.

The way in which the firm goes about this task is also important. The centralization considered necessary for ascertaining all types of risks and alternatives can be achieved in more than one way if strict guidelines for coordination are developed. The corporation must first designate clear responsibility for exposure management; one way to do so is to make the finance department a true profit centre with direct attribution of foreign exchange gains and losses and hedging costs, as well as certain interest costs and yields. Even here, it is further necessary to decide if the hedging or risk-acceptance decision will be the responsibility of a single designated individual or a committee, to delineate the role of foreign financial personnel and generally to organize the effort correctly. The role of regional headquarters can be an effective complement to the whole process, if in fact a dialogue is created in which the experience and perceptions of more than one source of expertise can be comingled. Any independent action by subsidiaries should not be undertaken without central approval.

Due to the complexity of the area, the amount of data to be assimilated and the function of probability, mathematical/computer application is of major interest. For compilation and permutation of statistical data, the computer is increasingly useful, as it also is in simple simulation models. Because of the unpredictability of short-term rates in the exchange markets and the unknown covariances between spot rates and interest rates, the more ambitious optimization programs have not been very successful to date.

From this description of foreign exchange exposure management, it has become clear that it must be closely integrated with its counterpart of liquidity management. Both deal with the monetary assets and liabilities of the firm, as well as factors which underlie them. The structural borrowing/investment policy setting in liquidity management can be seen to be the converse of a structural hedging/risk-acceptance policy in its sister area. Together, both form the conceptual area of global working capital management; success in either is essential for success in the other.

The need to integrate all aspects of finance, rather than to treat exposure as an autonomous problem, is even more clearly seen when tax policy is considered. The framework of both is identical, in their being constricted by outside regulatory bodies, in dealing with a fragmented and uncertain environment and in aiming to maximize the net income of the firms. The two management areas are anticipatory and require centralized decision-making. Given the particular importance of optimizing the tax decision, the input of tax implications of every foreign exchange tactic or in general strategy planning is essential.

The firm should also consider the broader effects of centralized exchange risk management on its personnel abroad, since it is they who may be most directly affected and whose expertise and goodwill lie at the basis of successful programmes.

To summarize the central tenets of this volume, the international corporation dealing with exchange risk should:

(1) Make its exposure management anticipatory, based on a perception of future risk as well as present positions.

(2) Centralize control over exposure risk as far as possible.

(3) Review its reporting systems as regards their adequacy and timeliness.

(4) Cover economic, transactional exposures generally and translation risk when the maximum potential translation losses are considered to be unacceptable by whatever corporate criteria are definitive. This implies a selective coverage policy, not one of being completely covered at all times in all currencies.

(5) Analyse and make exposure decisions on a post-tax basis.

(6) Look sceptically at exchange rate forecasting which provides one-point or very narrow-band estimates of future spot rates, just as sceptically at massive computer simulation programs which claim to simplify the decision-making decision.

(7) Coordinate exchange management closely with liquidity management, as both have common goals and are equally affected by environmental and structural constraints.

(8) Consider making the Head Office finance department a profit centre in its own right.

(9) Be aware of the non-financial implications of exposure strategy, particularly the personnel effects of centralization and the necessity to deal with an array of governmental and institutional contacts.

Installation of an exchange exposure management along these principles will allow a structured approach to an increasingly complex and critical area and complement the optimal development of International Money Management within the firm. The benefits of a more consistent approach, if adopted by all multinationals, would be seen not only on a micro-economic scale, but on the macro-economic plane of more orderly markets in general.

Appendix

The following is Appendix C of the Financial Accounting Standards Board Exposure Draft of December 31, 1974. It represents sections 46 through 145 of that Draft.

APPENDIX C

Basis for Conclusions

46. This Appendix discusses factors deemed significant by members of the Board in reaching the conclusions in this Statement, including various alternatives considered and reasons for accepting some and rejecting others.

Objective of Translation

47. The Board determined that to reach conclusions regarding the unique problems of translating foreign currency transactions and foreign statements, it should first identify the objective of the translation process.

48. Letters of comment received, personal views of task force members, and thoughts expressed in various writings on the subject have suggested the following objectives which were considered by the Board.

A. To present the financial statements of the enterprise in conformity with the generally accepted accounting principles that would apply had all assets, liabilities, revenue and expenses been measured and recorded in the reporting currency.
B. To retain in the enterprise's financial statements the accounting principles that are accepted in the foreign country for assets, liabilities, revenue and expenses measured and recorded in foreign currency.
C. To use a single unit of measure — a unit of the reporting currency — for financial statements that include translated foreign amounts; that is, to measure in the reporting currency, as well as to express in the reporting currency, assets, liabilities,

revenue or expenses that are measured or denominated in foreign currency.

D. To express in the reporting currency assets, liabilities, revenue and expenses measured in foreign currency but to retain the foreign currency as the unit of measure.

E. To produce an exchange gain or loss that is compatible with the expected economic effect of a rate change on business activities conducted in a currency other than the reporting currency.

U.S. or Foreign Accounting Principles (Objective A vs. Objective B)

49. Unless the same accounting principles are generally accepted in both the U.S. and the countries in which foreign operations are located, Objectives A and B are mutually exclusive. The translation process cannot retain both if the principles are different. One view is that the only meaningful foreign statements for translation purposes are those based on accounting principles generally accepted in the foreign country. This would suggest that if the attribute of an asset is measured on a basis not in conformity with U.S. generally accepted accounting principles, that measurement basis should, nonetheless, be retained in the translation process.

50. The opposing view is that U.S. generally accepted accounting principles have been developed and are well-known. Accordingly, readers of dollar financial statements, although perhaps not cognizant of all the principles used to prepare the statements, generally understand what the statements represent. Therefore, it is inappropriate to combine in the enterprise's financial statements accounts that represent similar assets and liabilities but that are measured by different accounting principles.

51. After considering the alternatives, the Board believes that it should require the concept that has been implicitly understood and applied in practice, namely that all financial statements included in consolidated financial statements should be prepared in conformity with U.S. generally accepted accounting principles. The Board believes that consistency of accounting procedures and measurement processes between foreign and domestic operations is desirable in the consolidation of foreign and domestic accounts. Therefore, foreign statements for purposes of combination, consolidation or equity accounting should be prepared in conformity with U.S. generally accepted accounting principles and translation should not change the measurement bases used in those foreign statements. The Board, therefore, accepted Objective A and rejected Objective B.

Single or Multiple Units of Measure (Objective C vs. Objective D)

52. Objectives C and D are also mutually exclusive. The translation process cannot retain both the reporting currency and the foreign

currency as the unit of measure following a rate change. For example, if an asset is acquired either by a foreign operation or a domestic operation for FC100 when the rate is FC1 = $1, its historical cost measured in either foreign currency or dollars can be expressed as $100 in the dollar financial statements. However, if the rate changes to FC1 = $2, the historical cost of the asset would be expressed as $200 (translated at the current rate) in the dollar financial statements to retain the foreign currency as the unit of measure. Expressing the cost as $100 after the rate change measures the historical cost of the asset in dollars, not in foreign currency.

53. The unit-of-measure issue focuses principally on the assets and liabilities of foreign operations that are measured at past prices in foreign currency.[1] There is general agreement that cash, receivables and payables measured or denominated in foreign currency, and assets and liabilities measured at current or future prices in foreign currency are translated at the current rate regardless of which currency is considered the unit of measure.[2]

54. The Board considered the purpose of consolidated financial statements under present generally accepted accounting principles in assessing whether or not the dollar or the foreign currency should be the appropriate unit of measure for foreign statements included in an enterprise's financial statements. *ARB No. 51*, 'Consolidated Financial Statements,' paragraph 1, states:

> The purpose of consolidated statements is to present, primarily for the benefit of the shareholders and creditors of the parent company, the results of operations and the financial position of a parent company and its subsidiaries essentially as if the group were a single company with one or more branches or divisions.

55. The Board believes that to be consistent with that purpose the translation process should reflect the transactions of the entire group, including foreign operations, as though the transactions were of a single enterprise. When an enterprise purchases an entity, the cost of the investment to the enterprise establishes the cost for the assets acquired for consolidated financial statements regardless of the acquired entity's existing book basis. Therefore, even though the acquired entity may have its own recorded cost for an asset, the enterprise's cost governs in the consolidation process.

56. The dollar is usually the unit of measure for financial statements of a U.S. entity, and there is no controversy regarding the cost of an asset acquired by a U.S. company in a foreign currency transaction that is settled at the rate in effect at the transaction date. *Cost* is measured in dollars at the transaction date, and that cost does not subsequently change as a result of rate changes. Although advocates of a one-

transaction perspective (see paragraph 67) have a different view of what constitutes cost, if settlement is at a rate different from the one in effect at the transaction date, they nevertheless recognize the dollar as the unit of measure.

57. Choosing the particular foreign currency to be the unit of measure for foreign operations that are included in dollar financial statements creates a practical problem, that is, selecting the particular currency for measuring the cost of an asset. For example, if an oil tanker is acquired at a price negotiated in Japanese yen and its cost is recorded in accounting records that use the U.S. dollar as the unit of measure, the dollar cost of that asset remains constant regardless of rate changes (see paragraph 56). If, however, the cost is measured and recorded in the accounting records of a foreign operation and translation retains the foreign currency as the unit of measure, the cost of the tanker reported in the dollar statements would change with changes in the dollar rate for that foreign currency. That is true regardless of the currency used to acquire the asset or the currency in which revenue from use of the asset will be generated. Thus, the tanker could be used to transport oil from the Middle East to France (and other European countries) and the revenue generated thereby might be stated in French francs (or other European currencies). Under those circumstances, the historical cost of that asset in the translated dollar financial statements would fluctuate with changes in the dollar rate for, say, the pound sterling simply if that is the local currency in which the cost of the tanker was originally measured and recorded.

58. Another example that also illustrates the potential consequences of selecting the local currency of a foreign operation as the unit of measure involves goodwill. If a U.S. parent acquires for cash a foreign operation located in Germany at a price in excess of the fair value of the net assets acquired, the difference is recognized as goodwill. If the acquisition is recorded in the parent's accounting records, the goodwill is measured in dollars and it would not change solely because of a rate change. If, however, the parent's Swiss subsidiary acquires the interest with the proceeds of a Euro-dollar borrowing or financing from the parent and records the investment in the Swiss accounts, the basis for the same goodwill reported in the dollar statements would change with changes in the dollar rate for the Swiss franc even though it does not change in the Swiss accounts. In other words, the translated cost in dollars of assets could be affected by discretionary selection of the accounting records in which the assets are recorded.

59. Since attempting to use a foreign currency as the unit of measure both produces results not in conformity with generally accepted accounting principles and creates a practical problem, the Board concluded that the units of measure should be the reporting currency of the enterprise and not the local currency of the foreign operation.

To use more than one unit of measure in the financial statements raises conceptual questions as to the description of the results. Thus, the Board rejected Objective D and adopted Objective C.

Compatibility (Objective E)

60. In its deliberations on each of several translation methods, the Board considered the views of respondents to the Discussion Memorandum and others who suggested, directly or indirectly, that the translation method should produce an exchange gain or loss that is compatible with the expected economic effects of a rate change. That is, the translation method should produce an exchange gain when the economic effect appears to be beneficial and an exchange loss when the economic effect appears to be detrimental.

61. A major problem with that objective is that to determine whether a translation method produces a compatible exchange or loss, one must first be able to ascertain the expected future economic effects of a rate change. The proposal seems to rest significantly on a general assumption that a local currency's strengthening is beneficial and its weaking is detrimental.

62. First, many interrelated and interacting forces are involved in a rate change. It is difficult, if not impossible, under most circumstances to predict with reasonable certainty the general effects of a rate change. A foreign operation in a country that experiences a major rate change may be affected both directly and indirectly by the adaptations and shifts that occur in that country's economy as a result of the currency adjustment. The nature and effect of those adaptations and modifications depend on a complex relation among factors, such as the relative degree to which general demand for imports and exports responds to changes in the foreign exchange price, the level of income and employment, the rate of economic expansion, monetary and fiscal policies instituted by the country whose currency has either weakened or strengthened, and conditions and forces existing in countries that are major trading partners. Accordingly, a foreign operation may experience complex changes in the local market demand and market price for its goods, changes in its local cost of goods and services procured, and in the local availability and cost of financing. Moreover, not all operations in the same environment will be affected in the same way because of differences in activities and realignments of price and cost structures within the local economy. To assess the expected economic effect of a rate change on a foreign operation's investment in plant and equipment, and possibly other long-lived assets, requires an economic forecast covering the lives of the assets.

63. Second, a foreign operation's exposure to the effect of a rate change may go beyond its recorded assets and liabilities. A foreign operation's unrecorded exposure to rate changes might include, for

example, sales and purchase backlog commitments at fixed foreign prices or fixed foreign currency streams of revenue or expense, such as interest or rent payments.

64. The proposed objective is impractical because foresight would be required to identify the future economic effects of a rate of change at the time it occurs.

65. Further, consistent application of the proposal would require changes in accounting for some U.S. operations with foreign currency transactions. For example, assume that a U.S. exporter has a foreign currency long-term borrowing and that as a result of the dollar's weakening, the exporter incurs an exchange loss on that debt. If, however, the economic effect of the rate change appears to be beneficial to his overall operations, the exporter's assets (which are measured and recorded in dollars) might require adjustment to produce a net gain that would be compatible with the expected future economic effect of the rate change.

66. The Board believes that present financial accounting and reporting reflects primarily the effects of past transactions and existing conditions, not future transactions or conditions. The translation process should not in and of itself, change the accounting model presently in use. Therefore, Objective E was rejected as an objective of the translation process.

Foreign Currency Transactions
Import/Export of Goods or Services

67. The Board's conclusions on accounting for foreign currency transactions reflect a two-transaction perspective. That perspective holds that when there is a foreign currency exchange exposure (exchange exposure) on a sale or purchase requiring settlement in foreign currency, the results, if any, of that exchange exposure should be accounted for separately from sales, cost of sales or inventory. A rate change does not affect previously recorded revenue from exports or the cost of imported goods or services. An alternate view, referred to as a one-transaction perspective, is that a transaction involving purchase or sale of goods or services with the price stated in foreign currency is incomplete until the amount in local currency (dollars) necessary to liquidate the related payable or receivable is determined. The amount recorded in dollars initially as cost or revenue is considered to be an estimate until final settlement. According to this view, an exchange gain or loss related to the transaction should be treated as an adjustment of the cost of imports or revenue from exports.

68. The Board considered and rejected the one-transaction perspective, described above. A purchase or sale with a price stated in a foreign currency involves essentially two transactions: a purchase or sale of an

asset and a commitment to buy or receive foreign currency. Specifically, the Board rejected the idea that the cost of an asset or the amount to be reported as revenue from exports is affected by later changes in the related liability or receivable.

69. The primary difference between a foreign currency transaction of an importer/exporter and a similar local currency transaction is that the former requires settlement in a foreign currency while the latter requires settlement in dollars. Thus, foreign currency transactions involve an exchange exposure that is not present in local currency transactions. The exchange gain or loss that may result from the exchange exposure is the result of an event (a rate change) that is separate from the original transaction. Since an exchange exposure can usually be eliminated by any of several actions, a determination not to avoid that exchange exposure should be accounted for by recognizing the gain or loss that results from that decision.

70. An implementation issue that arises under the two-transaction perspective is whether to establish the reporting currency basis of a transaction on (1) the date of a firm commitment to buy or sell at a foreign currency price or (2) on the transaction date.

71. The Board believes that recognizing exchange gains and exchange losses (as distinguished from net losses on firm purchase commitments[3]) on a commitment date basis could be both impracticable and inconsistent with the timing of recognizing the underlying transaction in the financial statements. For example, under present generally accepted accounting principles, both the purchaser and seller of raw material under a long-term supply contract would recognize costs and revenue, respectively, in their accounts on a performance basis. Since that kind of agreement might be considered a commitment, an enterprise that is party to a 5-year supply contract requiring payments in a foreign currency could conceivably have a significant exchange gain or loss if the total future payments were considered on a commitment basis. Since the supplier recognizes revenue and operating profit over the life of the contract, it would be inconsistent for him to accrue the expected effect of a rate change on future income. Likewise, an enterprise that must pay foreign currency for its raw materials could also have a significant exchange gain or loss, but its immediate recognition (except as otherwise required[4]) would be inappropriate for similar reasons.

72. Morevoer, a commitment date basis could present implementation problems because various degrees of commitment prior to consummation of a business transaction are possible. For example, a non-cancellable sales contract negotiated in a foreign currency might be considered by some as a reasonable basis on which to recognize an exchange gain or loss. However, a firm commitment to provide goods or services might require a commitment by the seller to purchase goods or

services in foreign currency to fulfill his obligation. Both commitments would need to be considered to reflect properly exchange gains and losses on a commitment date basis, but the purchase obligations might not necessarily be in the form of fixed contractual commitments.

Import/Export of Capital

73. The Board's conclusions on accounting for foreign currency transactions as they relate to the import or export of capital reflect a two-transaction perspective because the result of an exchange exposure is recognized separately. An alternate treatment considered by the Board was based on a one-transaction perspective similar to that described in paragraph 67. Pursuant to that view, an exchange gain or loss related to a loan payable denominated in foreign currency would be an adjustment of the cost of assets purchased with the borrowed funds. The Board's reasoning in rejecting a one-transaction perspective for the import of capital is similar to that stated in paragraphs 68 and 69.

74. Another possibility in accounting for the import or export of capital is to treat an exchange gain or loss related to a loan receivable or payable denominated in foreign currency as an adjustment of the cost of borrowing or the return from lending. Following that concept, an enterprise ideally would match exchange gains or losses against the cost or return from funds borrowed or loaned by using the interest method to amortize expected exchange gains or losses on principal and interest over the life of the debt or receivable. Since, at the date of a lending or borrowing, it is impossible to predict the rates that will prevail during the life of the loan, prospective (and partially retroactive) methods have been suggested for amortizing any exchange gain or loss. The Board rejected those methods for the reasons stated in paragraph 77.

Implementation

75. The Board believes that the accounting treatment specified in paragraph 8 offers more practical implementation than would a one-transaction perspective because it does not require, as does the one-transaction perspective, the tracing of exchange gains or losses on foreign currency payables or receivables to related assets, revenue or expenses. Another implementation problem under the one-transaction perspective is that a purchase or sale of goods or services may take place in one accounting period and an exchange gain or loss on the related payable or receivable may occur in a subsequent period.

Timing

76. The Board concluded that an exchange gain or loss shall be recorded when a rate change occurs. Two alternate answers considered

and rejected are to record an exchange gain or loss: (i) when payables or receivables are settled or (ii) when the rate changes more than a specified percentage from the rate previously used.

77. The Board's view is that a special situation exists when an enterprise is party to a foreign currency transaction, namely, the enterprise is subject to a gain or loss solely as a result of a rate change. Accordingly, when the rate changes, an exchange gain or loss resulting from the adjustment of accounts denominated in foreign currency should be immediately included in the determination of net income so as to properly report the results of that situation at the time it occurs. Financial statement users are thus informed of the results of a rate change in the period of change rather than at settlement in a later period, which might be many years after the rate change. Methods that involve amortizing exchange gains or losses also fail to recognize the effect of a rate change in the period of occurrence and are, therefore, also rejected. (Also, see paragraph 121.)

78. The possibility of recording exchange gains or losses only if the rate changes more than a specified percentage was also considered and rejected. Any allowable percentage range within which rates might fluctuate without being reflected in the financial statements would, of necessity, be arbitrary. In addition, since a relatively minor change in a rate could sometimes have a material impact on the financial statements, depending on the size of the enterprise's position in the foreign currency involved, the method could produce misleading results. Thus, the Board concluded that the rate to be used at the balance sheet date should be the current rate.

79. The Board also considered the view that an exchange gain or loss should be deferred if there was the likelihood that a rate change might reverse. The argument is that not doing so creates fluctuations in income by reporting exchange gains or losses that are cancelled by reversals or rate changes. However, since to predict the rates that will exist in the future is impossible,[5] the Board concluded that the proper accounting to use the current rate and include exchange gains or losses currently in the income statement.

Foreign Statements

80. Paragraphs 80—100 compare the following normative methods for translating assets and liabilities measured in foreign currency against the objective of translation adopted by the Board (a situational approach to the application of these methods is discussed in paragraphs 101—110).

(a) Current rate method.
(b) Current-non-current method.

(c) Monetary-non-monetary method.

(d) Temporal method.

The principal distinction among various normative methods of translation is the requirement to translate particular classifications of assets and liabilities at either the current or historical rate.

Current Rate Method

81. The current rate method translates all assets and liabilities at the current rate.

82. The Board believes that the attributes of a foreign operation's assets and liabilities should be measured in the foreign statements in conformity with generally accepted accounting principles applicable for the reporting enterprise and that those principles should be retained in the translation process (see paragraph 51). If assets and liabilities that are measured at past prices in foreign statements are translated at the current rate and included in dollar financial statements, the dollar financial statements depart from historical-cost-based accounting because property, plant, equipment and other assets normally carried at cost are reflected at varying dollar amounts resulting from changes in rates. The dollar amounts would not, except by coincidence, consistently represent any measurement basis.

83. A contrary view has been expressed that the historical cost of an asset acquired by a foreign operation can be measured only in the foreign currency. That view holds that there is no historical dollar cost for such an asset. Translating the foreign currency historical cost of an asset into a fewer or greater number of dollars following a rate change is simply the result of an absolute, mathematical revision in the rate and thus does not represent a departure from the historical-cost principle of accounting; the foreign currency cost is the only historical cost, and that cost has not changed.

84. Although an asset's acquisition price may have been stated in a particular currency, its equivalent cost in another currency can be approximated by multiplying the stated currency price by the rate in effect at the date of acquisition. Just as the length of an object can be measured in inches and then remeasured in centimetres by applying the appropriate conversion rate, the *cost* of an asset can likewise be measured in various units of measure (different currencies) by applying the appropriate translation rates.

85. Accordingly, the Board rejected the view that historical cost can be measured only in the foreign currency. It also rejected the current rate method for the reason stated in paragraph 82.

Current-Non-current Method

86. The current-non-current method generally translates current

assets and liabilities at the current rate and non-current assets and liabilities at applicable historical rates. As illustrated in the two succeeding paragraphs the method deviates from the objectives adopted by the Board most significantly in translating inventory and long-term debt.

87. Inventory carried at historical cost in foreign statements is generally translated at the current rate using the current-non-current method. As indicated in paragraph 82, that translation results in a departure from historical-cost-based accounting measured in dollars. Later changes in market prices or rates cannot change the historical cost of an asset already owned. Once recorded, the historical cost of an asset can be amortized or otherwise charged to expense in accounting records but cannot be changed because of varying prices[6] without changing the basis of accounting from historical cost to something else.

88. As measured in local currency, long-term debt denominated in local currency and any related unamortized discount or premium represent the present value of future interest and principal payments based on the effective rate of interest as determined at the date the debt was incurred. If exchange rates change after that date, translating long-term debt and any related discount or premium at the historical rate, as required by the current-non-current method, does not retain this measurement basis. Translation at the historical rate produces a result that is unrelated to the current dollar equivalent of the present value, based on the effective rate of interest as determined at the date the debt was incurred, of the remaining future interest and principal payments. Furthermore, unless the rate change reverses before the debt is settled, translation at the historical rate merely serves to delay recognition of the exchange gain or loss — it does not avoid the gain or loss. (See paragraph 77 for additional reasons that long-term debt should be translated at the current rate.)

89. Existing definitions of current and non-current assets and liabilities contain nothing to explain why that classification scheme should determine the rate used to translate. The attributes of assets and liabilities that are measured in financial statements differ from their nature that determines their classification as current or non-current. Consequently, different kinds of assets or liabilities may be measured the same way but classified differently or classified the same way but measured differently. For example, under present generally accepted accounting principles both inventory and plant and equipment are measured at historical cost, but inventory is classified as a current asset and plant and equipment as non-current assets. Since translation is concerned with measurement and not with classification, the characteristics of assets and liabilities that determine their classification for purposes of disclosure are not relevant for selecting the rate for translation.

90. For the reasons set forth in paragraphs 87—89, the Board rejected the current-non-current method.

Monetary-Non-monetary Method

91. The monetary-non-monetary method generally translates monetary assets and liabilities at the current rate and non-monetary assets and liabilities at applicable historical rates. For translation purposes, assets and liabilities are monetary if they are expressed terms of a fixed number of foreign currency units. All other balance sheet items are classified as non-monetary.

92. The monetary-non monetary method suffers from the same type of deficiency as the current-non-current method, namely, that its classification scheme is inappropriate for invariably retaining the attributes of assets and liabilities being measured. Certain assets and liabilities have both monetary and non-monetary characteristics. For example, bonds and negotiable notes are contractual rights to fixed amounts of money (a monetary characteristic) but also have selling prices that can change (a non-monetary characteristic). Many bonds and notes, therefore, cannot be translated under the nonetary-non-monetary method unless the method is modified to require translation of these items according to whether the monetary or non-monetary attribute is to be measured in the financial statements. Although that modification is possible, it demonstrates a basic flow in the classification scheme for translation purposes.

93. No comprehensive principle of translation can be derived solely from the monetary-non-monetary distinction. Non-monetary assets and liabilities are measured on different bases (for example, past prices or current prices) under different circumstances; and translation at a past rate does not always fit. Translating non-monetary items at a past rate produces reasonable results if the items are stated at historical cost but not if they are stated at current market price in foreign currency. For example, if a foreign operation purchases as an investment 100 shares of another company's common stock (a non-monetary item) for FC1000 when the rate is FC1 = $1, the cost of that investment is equivalent to $1000. IF the investment is carried at cost by the foreign operation, treating the investment as a non-monetary item and translating it at the historical rate is appropriate. However, if the investment is carried at market price, translating that basis by the historical rate usually produces questionable results. For example, if the current market value of the investment is FC1500 and the current rate is FC1 = $1.25, translating FC1500 into $1500 using the historical rate does not result in the current market value measured in dollars (FC1500 x 1.25 = $1875) or the historical cost in dollars.

94. Although the deficiencies of the monetary-non-monetary method have been recognized and dealt with in practice, the Board found the

monetary-non-monetary method concept inadequate as a comprehensive method of translation.

95. Although supporting the monetary-non-monetary method, certain respondents to the Discussion Memorandum recommended that inventory carried at cost (on other than a LIFO basis) should be translated at the current rate if local currency selling prices are not immediately responsive to rate changes and the inventory turnover period is relatively short. It was advocated that translating inventory at the historical rate under such circumstances result in a distortion of the dollar gross profit during the inventory turnover period.

96. As indicated in paragraph 87, translating inventory carried at cost at the current rate departs from historical cost-based accounting. In addition, determining, particularly during a period of floating rates, whether or not selling prices are immediately responsive to rate changes could be impractical. Although applying historical rates may affect the dollar gross profit, the Board believes that is the expected result of using the dollar as the unit of measure in concert with generally accepted accounting principles. Therefore, he Boadrd rejected the recommendation set forth in the preceding paragraph.

Temporal Method

97. The temporal method, proposed by *ARS No. 12*, translates assets and liabilities carried at past, current or future prices expressed in foreign currency in a manner that retains the accounting principles used to measure them in the foreign statements; that is, the attributes of the assets and liabilities measured are the same after translation as before. Thus, the temporal method changes a measurement in foreign currency into a measurement in dollars without changing the basis of the measurement. The temporal method can therefore accommodate any basis of measurement — for example, historical cost, current replacement price or current selling price — that is based on dated exchanges. It thus achieves one of the objectives of translation which is to retain the measurement bases of foreign statement items (see paragraph 51).

98. The translation procedures to apply the temporal method are generally the same as those now used by U.S. enterprises under the monetary-non-monetary method. The results of the temporal method and the monetary-non-monetary method coincide because under present generally accepted accounting principles monetary assets and liabilities are usually measured at amounts that pertain to the balance sheet date and non-monetary assets and liabilities were acquired. The temporal principle thus provides a conceptual basis for the translation procedures that are now used to apply the monetary-non-monetary method which by itself does not contain an adequate basis for those procedures as indicated in paragraphs 92 and 93.

99. The coincidence of results between the temporal method and the

monetary-non-monetary method is due solely to the nature of present generally accepted accounting principles — assets and liabilities are measured on bases that coincide with their classifications as monetary and non-monetary. The results of the temporal method and the monetary-non-monetary method would differ significantly under other accounting principles that would require non-monetary assets and liabilities to be measured at prices in effect at dates other than those at which they were acquired or incurred.

100. The monetary-non-monetary method happens to produce appropriate translation results at the present time because of the nature of present generally accepted accounting principles. However, generally accepted accounting principles are subject to change and one of the changes that has been recommended is to require non-monetary assets to be stated at a current value — for example, current replacement price. The monetary-non-monetary method would not be appropriate under replacement price accounting because translation of the replacement price of a non-monetary asset at the effect when the asset was required produces translation results that cannot be meaningfully described except in terms of the computations made to obtain them. In contrast, the temporal method produces appropriate translation results under replacement price accounting and all other types of accounting based on exchange prices just as it does under historical cost accounting.

A Situational Approach to Translation

101. Paragraphs 81—100 compare the four basic normative methods for translating balance sheet accounts against the objectives of translation adopted by the Board. A somewhat different approach to translation has also been suggested which is not a normative method but rather looks at the nature of each foreign operation. It distinguishes between those foreign operations that are extensions of affiliated domestic operations, (*dependent* operations[7]) and those whose operations are essentially self-contained and therefore not dependent upon affiliated domestic operations (*independent* operations[7]). The situational argument is that since many factors influence the creation of a foreign operation, translation must look further than the location of a business operation; it should also look to its nature.

102. According to that view, if a foreign operation is dependent upon domestic operations, the foreign operation should be accounted for as an extension of those operations (that is, as part of a single domestic operation) and its foreign statements should be translated by one of the normative methods other than the current rate method. If a foreign operation is independent, its foreign statements should be translated using the current rate method.

103. A principal reason given to support using the current rate

method to translate independent foreign operations is that the assets and liabilities of those operations are not individually at risk to rate changes; rather, the entire business is at risk. Since the foreign activities are conducted entirely in a foreign environment and future cash flows will be in a foreign currency, it follows that future operating results can be expressed in a meaningful way in dollars only if all revenue and costs (including those carried forward from a period prior to the rate change) are translated at the current rate. From the enterprise's viewpoint, its net investment in the foreign operation represents its total exposure to a rate change. Only by translating the net assets of the foreign operation at the current rate can the effect of rate changes be properly measured.

104. Selective use of the current rate method to translate all assets and liabilities of foreign operations that are independent and the use of another method to translate all other foreign operations, would require the establishment of conditions to be met before the current rate method could be used. Although proponents of the approach have not discussed any specific criteria that might be applicable, the Board did consider but was unable to develop criteria that might determine that a foreign operation was independent.

105. Although there could be problems in consistently applying any set of criteria to determine independence (some of which are discussed in paragraph 109), the Board believes it is more appropriate to focus on the purpose that the distinction is apparently trying to achieve. While the operation of any business involves risk, an operation in a foreign country involves additional risks, one of which is the risk of rate changes. The Board believes that certain advocates of the situational approach are attempting to measure the exchange risk separately from other business risks. To do so, translation must therefore be *solely* a valuation process — the effect of the exchange risk is measured by valuing all assets and liabilities before and after movements in the rate; or viewed in a different perspective, a net investment in a foreign operation is an integrated whole on which the effect of a rate change can best be determined by multiplying the investment by the change in rate. If that view is correct, all independent foreign operations in a country whose currency weakens should be worth less (the net investment multiplied by the decline in the rate will produce an exchange loss) and, similarly, independent foreign operations in a country whose currency strengthens should be worth more.

106. However, given that historical-cost-based accounting is the basis for preparing financial statements, translation cannot be viewed solely as a valuation procedure that measures the overall gain or loss caused by a rate change. That conclusion results because multiplying the historical foreign currency cost of an asset by the current rate cannot, except by coincidence, measure the value of the asset. For example, an enterprise

in England acquired land in 1964 at a cost of 1,000,000 pounds sterling when the rate was £1 = $2.80; (the dollar equivalent historical cost is therefore $2,800,000). If the land being carried at cost in the foreign statements at December 31, 1974 is multiplied by the current rate £1 = 2.35, the product will be $2,350,000. However, the current dollar equivalent of the value of that land may be more or less than $2,350,000. If the purchase of the land was financed by locally incurred long-term debt due on December 31, 1974, translation over the 10-year period under the method advocated by this Statement would result in recognizing an aggregate $450,000 gain (excluding income tax consequences). Using the current rate method during the period would have resulted in no net gain or loss because the amount of the debt equalled the carrying basis (cost) of the asset or, treating the accounts individually, the gain on the debt offset the loss on the asset. Undeniably, a gain on the debt measured in dollars has occurred because it was liquidated at the equivalent of $2,350 000 while the equivalent proceeds received at the date incurred was $2,800,000. Whether or not the value of the land acquired has changed can only be ascertained by determining its current market price. To make the translation process solely one of valuation, that market price would also have to be recorded in the foreign statements before translation.

107. The assumption in the foregoing illustration was that the foreign operation was independent. If it were dependent, advocates of the situational approach agree that the $450,000 gain on the debt should be reflected in the determination of net income over the 10-year period (although they may not agree on the appropriate time of recognition) and that an exchange loss on the land should not be accounted for as a result of the weakening of the pound sterling. The Board believes that to calculate an exchange loss on an asset solely because of the *independence* of a foreign operation is inappropriate. Further, although the Board recognized that foreign operations may be structured differently, it could find no persuasive reasons why they should be translated differently.

108. Certain respondents to the Discussion Memorandum, recognizing the purpose of consolidated financial statements as set forth in paragraph 54, recommended that if the current rate method were deemed appropriate for certain foreign operations for the reasons set forth in paragraph 103, those operations should be accounted for under the equity method rather than line-by-line consolidation. The Board believes that adoption of that kind of recommendation raises broad questions about the concepts of consolidation and the equity method applicable to domestic as well as foreign operations that are beyond the scope of this Statement.

109. As indicated in paragraph 105, the Board believes there could be problems in applying any set of criteria to determine independence,

including whether foreign operations should be viewed on a foreign operation-by-foreign operation, country-by-country, or segment-by-segment basis (that is, each major segment of a foreign operation would be evaluated separately). In addition, changes in classification (from dependent to independent or vice versa) between reporting periods, presumably necessitating the use of different translation methods for each period, could produce results that would not be comparable with those of prior periods. It is also unclear how to translate the financial statements of a foreign operation that is dependent on another foreign economy (for example, a foreign operation manufacturers its product in various South American countries and sells its product to an affiliated, or unaffiliated, European operation).

110. Another suggestion is that if the current rate method is appropriate for operations located in highly inflationary economies (for example, some South American countries), the foreign statements should be first adjusted for the general price level effects of local inflation and then translated at the current rate because to do otherwise could produce unreasonable results in dollars. The Board believes that in addition to the problem of identifying *highly inflationary* economies, adjusting some part but not all of an enterprise's financial statements for general price level changes mixes the units of measure used in the financial statements and results in an aggregation of numbers that cannot be meaningfully described except in terms of the procedures followed to obtain them. That is, adding units of general purchasing power (the unit of measure used in general price level statements) translated at the current rate and units of money (the unit of measure used in conventional statements) produces a total that represents neither aggregate units of money nor aggregate units of general purchasing power.

Translation of Revenue and Expense Accounts

111. The Board believes that the transaction method, rather than the closing rate method, should be used to translate revenue and expense accounts because it satisfies one objective of translation the Board has adopted, namely, to measure transactions in the enterprise's reporting currency.

112. The closing rate method is linked to the view that the foreign currency should be retained as the unit of measure. Thus, translating revenue and expenses at the closing rate retains the foreign currency as the unit of measure for transactions occurring during the year (including those previously reported for interim periods). If the rate changes, dollar translations of prior local currency transactions during the current year are restated to reflect the new dollar equivalents of the transactions. Accordingly, no exchange gain or loss on the current year's transactions is separately recognized using the closing rate

method. Since the Board believes that the dollar, rather than the foreign currency, should be the unit of measure it rejected the closing rate method.

Determination of Exchange Gain or Loss

113. In theory, the exchange gain or loss from translating foreign statements is determined at the date the rate between the foreign currency and the dollar changes and is the difference between (a) the assets and liabilities of the foregn operation subject to adjustment (those consistently translated at the current rate) translated into dollars at the rate in effect before the rate change and (b) the same assets and liabilities translated into dollars at the rate in effect after the change.

114. In practice, however the exchange gain or loss is usually determined at the close of a period by translating both the ending balance sheet and income statement accounts at the rates (for example, current and historical rates for assets and liabilities and weighted average rate for revenue and expenses) required by a particular translation method or approach. When the translation is completed and the net income less dividends (in dollars) is added to the beginning dollar retained earnings balance, the sum of those amounts will usually not equal the ending dollar retained earnings shown in the translated balance sheet. The difference is an exchange gain or loss.

Disposition of Exchange Gain or Loss

115. The Board principally considered the following possible methods to account for exchange gains or losses in arriving at its conclusion stated in paragraph 14.

(a) Adjust cost of, or amortize over life of, assets carried at cost in dollars (assets translated at historical rate).
(b) Amortize over remaining term of long-term liabilities.
(c) Adjust stockholder's equity.
(d) Defer based on certain criteria.
(e) Include both immediately in the determination of net income.

Adjustment related to assets carried at cost

116. One view to support treating exchange gains and losses as adjustments of the cost basis of assets is that the cost of an asset equals the total sacrifice required to discharge all related liabilities. Accordingly, if a foreign operation has an exposed net liability position at the time of a rate change, the exchange gain or loss is an element of the cost of the related assets. That view is similar to a one-transaction perspective and is rejected for reasons similar to those set forth in paragraphs 68 and 69.

117. Another view is that when an exposed net liability position

exists, an exchange loss resulting from the strengthening of a foreign currency is considered *covered* in whole or in part by assets carried at cost. (The *cover* is the amount by which those assets if translated at the current rate would exceed their cost in dollars.) According to that argument, the *covered* loss should be deferred rather than included in the determination of net income when the rate changes. The amortization over the life of the assets of the deferred debit relating to the exposed net liability position is considered to be at least offset by the effect of the *lighter* costs (based on historical translation rates) that will increase earnings when the assets are charged to income at historical rates and generate assets (cash or receivables resulting from sales) translated at the current rate.

118. Likewise, if an exposed net liability position exists, an exchange gain resulting from a foreign currency's weakening should be deferred under the *cover* approach to the extent required to offset the unrecognized potential loss on the assets translated at the historical rate. The potential loss represents the difference between translation of the assets at the higher historical rates and translation at the lower current rate. This approach views translating the assets at historical rates as speculation regarding the assets' ability to produce a product that will sell for an increased foreign currency selling price which, when translated at the current rate, will sufficiently cover the historical dollar cost of the assets. Amortization of the deferred gain over the life of the assets is therefore considered appropriate to offset the effect of the *heavier* (historical) costs to be included in the determination of subsequent periods' net income.

119. In rejecting the cover approach, the Board viewed it as essentially a procedure whereby a change in the dollar equivalent of an exposed net liability position is offset (deferred) against a potential change in the future dollar value of assets carried at cost (the dollar value of such assets depends on the foreign currency proceeds generated when the assets enter into the determination of net income). Since changes in the value of assets carried at cost (for example, property, plant and equipment) are not normally recognized under generally accepted accounting principles until the assets are sold, offsetting is accomplished under the cover approach by *not* including immediately in the determination of net income gains or losses on changes in the dollar equivalent of an exposed net liability position. The argument for deferral is in effect that changes in the dollar equivalent of one item should not be recognized because changes in the dollar value of another item are not recognized. However, the Board believes that offsetting is not proper under present generally accepted accounting principles that recognize certain gains and losses when values change and others only at time of sale or other disposition. If offsetting is desirable at all, it should be accomplished by changing generally

accepted accounting principles to recognize changes in the dollar value of *both* items. However, to do so would require reconsideration of historical cost as a fundamental concept of accounting — a process that is beyond the scope of this Statement.

120. An apparent assumption of the cover approach is that future revenue generated by the assets carried at cost will be in the same currency as the exposed net liability position. That may not be true in all situations. In addition, the cover concept appears to presume that a rate change may be expected to affect future earnings in a way that offsets any exchange gain or loss related to an exposed net liability position. The Board believes that future impacts of rate changes should be reflected in the future and not anticipated by deferral of an exchange gain or loss.

Adjustment related to life of long-term liabilities

121. Another method that has been suggested would limit deferral of exchange gains or losses when an exposed net liability position exists to amounts associated with long-term liabilities denominated in foreign currency. The amount deferred would be amortized over the remaining term of such long-term liabilities. The method in effect accounts for the deferred exchange gain or loss as an adjustment of financing costs (interest expense). The Board rejected the method for reasons given in paragraphs 74 and 77 and because the method masks the economic difference in the source (denomination) of financing, that is, foreign currency denominated debt has an exchange exposure that dollar denominated debt or equity financing does not. Spreading the result of that exposure over the future rather than recognizing it in full when a rate changes fails to contrast an economic difference between financing denominated in foreign currency and dollar borrowings or equity financing.

Adjustment to stockholders' equity

122. Certain respondents to the Discussion Memorandum suggested that exchange gains or losses be accounted for as adjustments of stockholders' equity. The Board rejected that method because it believes that a gain or loss resulting from an exposure to rate changes should be included in the determination of net income in accordance with the all-inclusive income statement presently required by accordance with the all-inclusive income statement presently required by generally accepted accounting principles. A foreign investment exposes a U.S. company to the effects of rate changes which can be economically beneficial or detrimental. The Board believes that those benefits or detriments should be reflected in the determination of net income at a time and in a manner that is consistent with generally accepted accounting principles.

Deferral based on certain criteria

123. The following criteria have been suggested for deferring exchange gains and/or losses.

(a) Realization
(b) Conservatism
(c) Likelihood of reversal of rate change
(d) The effect on future income of rate change.

124. It has been suggested that exchange gains or losses be deferred based on the criterion of realization. Realized gains and losses should be recognized immediately while unrealized gains and (possibly) losses should be deferred until realized. In the Board's view, the distinction between *realized* and *unrealized* exchange gains and losses is a questionable concept for the purpose of translation as well as a difficult concept to implement.

125. If transmission of funds (for example, dividends) from the foreign operation to a domestic operation is the event that determines *realization* of exchange gains and losses from translating foreign statements, it is questionable how that event causes an exchange gain or loss to be realized. For example, an exchange gain that results from translating a foreign operation's exposed net liability position cannot be reasonably associated with a dividend remittance. Likewise, an exchange gain that results from translating a foreign operation's **exposed net asset position** that primarily reflects accounts receivable cannot be reasonably associated with a dividend remittance if the foreign currency collected on settlement of the receivables is used to purchase other assets. If remittance of dividends were the criterion for realization, then perhaps all of a foreign operation's earnings would be considered *unrealized*.

126. If, rather than the transmission of funds, the collection of receivables and payment of payables in existence at the date of a rate change were the events that determined realization of an exchange gain or loss, determining the composition of balance sheets at the dates rates changed and then tracing those items to their ultimate settlement would be impractical. Further, the Board saw no theoretical justification for this distinction between realized and unrealized exchange gains or losses (see paragraph 132).

127. Another suggestion is that unrealized exchange gains should be deferred based on the criterion of conservatism. The Board believes that in addition to the difficulty of determining unrealized exchange gains, recognizing unrealized exchange losses while deferring unrealized exchange gains is an unwarranted inconsistency within the translation process.

128. Although the concept of conservatism may be appropriate in

other areas of accounting, the Board believes its application to translation of foreign statements is inappropriate. A rate change provides sufficient objective evidence to warrant changes in the dollar carrying amount of cash, receivables, payables and other assets and liabilities measured in foreign currency at current or future prices. To defer an exchange gain solely because it is a *gain* would in effect deny that a rate change has occurred.

129. The Board rejected the recommendation that exchange gains or losses be deferred if rates are likely to reverse. Given the high degree of unpredictability in exchange rates, that method creates a situation in which operating results are misstated simply through errors in forecasting. A procedure of that type would invariably cause divergent decisions about the movements or rates. In addition, to determine how much of an exchange gain or loss will be reversed when the rate change reverses would also necessitate a forecast of the financial position at the time of the later rate change which may be another extremely uncertain variable.

130. Another recommendation proposed that accounting for exchange gains or losses vary depending on the likely effect of rate changes on future income. As pointed out in paragraphs 62—64, the future effects of rate changes may vary widely and the effects are uncertain. Consequently, the Board believes it inappropriate to inject forecasting of future effects into the accounting for exchange gains or losses.

Additional factors considered

131. An additional factor in the Board's decision to include exchange gains or losses in the determination of net income at the time of a rate change is that, in general, deferral approaches raise significant questions of implementation. For example, should amounts deferred be determined on a global, currency-by-currency, country-by-country, foreign operation-by-foreign operation, or some other basis? If exchange gains or losses are aggregated on a global basis, most suggested amortization approaches become exceedingly complex, if not impractical, to apply by a company with numerous foreign operations. Not aggregating on a global basis can result in exchange gains being included in the determination of net income at the time of a rate change and exchange losses being deferred or vice versa depending on the deferral method employed.

132. Another factor that supports including exchange gains or losses in the determination of net income at the time of a rate change is that after a rate change operating revenue (other than amortization of deferred income) as well as other cash receipts and disbursements are translated at the current rate. To recognize the effect of a rate change on current transactions (by reporting in the translated statements an

increased or decreased dollar equivalent for the transactions) when they occur and yet defer the effect of a rate change on past unsettled transactions (for example, receivables from previously reported sales) is inconsistent.

Income Tax Consequences of Rate Changes

133. The Board concluded that if an exchange gain or loss related to a foreign currency transaction of a foreign operation is taxable in the foreign country, the related tax effect shall be included in the translated income statement when the rate change occurs. Such inclusion is appropriate regardless of the fact that the foreign operation's exchange gain or loss may be partially or completely (in the case of a dollar denominated asset or liability) eliminated upon translation, because the rate change is the event that causes the tax effect in the foreign operation's financial statements. The fact that the exchange gain or loss does not exist (or exists only partially) in terms of dollars should in no way affect the accounting for the tax effect, which does exist in terms of dollars.

134. A method has been proposed for measuring exchange gains or losses resulting from translating foreign statements that in effect would correct what might be considered a distorted relationship of translated tax expense to translated pre-tax income. Following the proposal, the exchange gain or loss would include the future tax effect in the translated financial statements of using the historical rate for translating inventory, plant and equipment. The resulting deferred tax accounts would be amortized as an adjustment of tax expense as inventory and fixed assets are charged against operations.

135. The Board does not believe that the use of historical rates to translate certain income or expense items (for example, cost of goods sold and depreciation) requires interperiod tax allocation. Timing differences, defined as 'differences between the periods in which transactions affect taxable income and the periods in which they enter into the determination of pretax accounting income' (paragraph 13(e) of *APB Opinion No. 11*), do not arise from translating assets or liabilities at historical rates. Accordingly, the effective tax rate in the translated dollar statements may differ from the effective tax rate in the foreign statements. Applying historical rates may also change various other relationships in the translated dollar statements from those in the foreign statements (for example, gross profit percentages). However, the Board believes that is the expected result of using the dollar as the unit of measure in concert with generally accepted accounting principles.

136. As to whether or not U.S. deferred taxes should be accrued for exchange gains or losses resulting from the translation of foreign statements into dollars, the Board concluded that the existing authori-

tative literature (*APB Opinions No. 11, 23 and 24*) provides sufficient guidance in this area.

Forward Exchange Contracts

137. A forward exchange contract (forward contract) is an agreement to exchange at a future date currencies of different countries at a specified exchange rate (the forward rate). A forward contract may be related to a specific import/export transaction (goods, services, or capital), be related to a foreign currency exposed net asset or net liability position, or be speculative in anticipation of a gain.

138. Initially, a forward contract has no economic value. One can act either as a buyer or seller of the same currency for the same maturity (at only a slight rate difference represented by the dealer's *spread*). Subsequently, forward contracts gain economic substance as one party or the other is incorrect in his assessment of the future spot rate. Before contract maturity, the market value is determined by the difference between the forward rate in the contract and the rate available for the remaining maturity of the forward contract. At contract maturity, the difference between the then spot rate and the contracted forward rate determines the ultimate economic value for the forward contract.

139. The Board believes that the difference between original market value of a forward contract (zero) and its current market value should be accrued. Stated another way, the difference between the contracted forward rate and the forward rate available for the remaining maturity of that forward contract multiplied by the amount of the forward contract is a gain or loss. Since (a) movement of spot rates affect forward rates and (b) forward contracts may be used to hedge against exposed foreign currency positions, the Board concluded that accrued gains and losses on forward contracts should be included in the determination of net income currently. To do otherwise (that is, to recognize gains and losses only at maturity) could result in benefiting (penalizing) one period's income statement by recognizing an exchange gain (loss) resulting from the translation process currently to the detriment (benefit) of a subsequent period's income statement when a loss (gain) on the forward contract is recorded.

140. An alternative approach for forward contracts related to specific import/export transactions which have transpired is to use the rate in a forward contract rather than the spot rate to establish the related amounts payable or receivable for the imports or exports. Although a forward contract may limit or eliminate exposure on a payable or receivable denominated in foreign currency, the Board views forward contracts as independent transactions that should be accounted for separately. Accruing changes in the market value of the forward contract results in the same net effect on the determination of net

income as does the alternative approach. Since specific identification of individual forward contracts with related import/export transactions may not always be possible, the accrual procedure is the more practical approach.

Disclosure

141. In reaching its conclusion regarding disclosures, the Board considered disclosures required by *FASB Statement No. 1* as well as additional possible disclosures presented in the Discussion Memorandum.

142. Since this Statement specifies a single accounting method for foreign currency translation, the Board concluded that the disclosure requirements as stated in *FASB Statement No. 1* are no longer appropriate.

143. Paragraph 20 herein requires disclosure of the aggregate exchange gain or loss and the aggregate related tax effect included in the determination of net income for the period. An exchange gain or loss does not measure, nor is it necessarily an indicator of, the full economic effect of a rate change on an enterprise. The disclosure required by paragraph 20 provides information to users of financial statements about the effects of rate changes on certain assets and liabilities which may be useful in evaluating and comparing reported results of operations.

144. The Board considered and rejected a requirement to disclose the effect of rate changes on sales and earnings. As indicated in paragraphs 62 and 63, it may be difficult or impossible to quantify the economic effects of rate changes (for example, on selling prices, sales volume, and cost structures). In the Board's opinion, disclosure of the effects of translating revenue and expenses at rates different from those used in a preceding period could be misleading unless other significant direct and indirect economic effects of rate changes on operations are considered and disclosed. Thus, the Board concluded that since the effect of rate changes on sales and earnings cannot always be measured with a sufficient degree of precision, it could not require disclosures of that type. The Board noted, however, that some companies have disclosed certain information (not necessarily in financial statements) that might be interpreted as showing the effect of rate changes on sales and earnings. The Board's intention is not to preclude or discourage those disclosures in financial statements if, in the opinion of management, the disclosures represent useful information. However, the Board believes that if those disclosures are made, it is essential that, as required by paragraph 21 of this Statement, a clear explanation of the methods and underlying assumptions used to determine such amounts also be disclosed in the financial statements.

145. Chapter 12 of *ARB No. 43* states, 'it is important that especial

care be taken to make full disclosure in the financial statements of United States companies of the extent to which they include significant foreign items' (paragraph 6) and 'adequate disclosure of foreign operations should be made' (paragraph 8). The disclosure of geographical, or otherwise segmented, information on foreign operations is being considered in the FASB project, 'Financial Reporting for Segments of a Business Enterprise'. Accordingly, until resolution of that project, the aforementioned portions of Chapter 12 remain in effect. The other paragraphs of Chapter 12 of *ARB No. 43* not superseded by this Statement deal with matters beyond the scope of this Statement.

Notes

1. There is another important theoretical distinction between the two opposing views involving the way in which the effect of the translation process is recognized. If the dollar is the unit of measure, a change in the carrying amounts of some assets and liabilities resulting from a rate change affects net income. If, however, the foreign currency is the unit of measure in dollar statements of foreign operations, prior dollar-translated statements need to be restated to current equivalent dollars to make them comparable with current translated statements. Restatement would not change the prior periods' statements in any way except to update the amounts to current equivalent dollars.
2. There is, however, debate as to when the current rate should be applied. See paragraphs 31, 41 and 43.
3. *ARB No. 43*, Chapter 4, Statement 10, reads: 'Accrued net losses on firm purchase commitments for goods for inventory, measured in the same way as are inventory losses, should, if material, be recognized in the accounts...'. An enterprise could have an exchange loss on a commitment to acquire or sell inventory which might reduce its operating profit but not cause a net loss when sold.
4. See Note 3.
5. To apply the suggested alternative method properly, it would be necessary to know in advance both future rates and the changes in an enterprise's exposure to rate changes that will occur during the period prior to reversal of the rate movement.
6. An exchange rate can be considered the price of a dollar in another currency. Multiplying the foreign currency cost of an asset by a new rate does not, except perhaps by coincidence, result in a measurement that is either current replacement cost or selling price.
7. The terms *dependent* and *independent* were used by Parkinson and are used in the same context here. (Parkinson, R. MacDonald, *Translation of Foreign Currencies*, Toronto: Institute of Chartered Accountants, 1972.)

Glossary

Appreciation, Exchange
An increase in the value of a given currency in terms of other currencies.

Arbitrage, Exchange
The simultaneous purchase or sale of a foreign currency in two or more locations to take advantage of differing spot rates and to achieve thereby a profit from those differentials.

Arbitrage, Interest
Taking advantage of differing rates of interest in two countries, normally by borrowing in one country and lending or investing in another.

Authorized Dealer (or Authorized Bank)
A bank in the United Kingdom or other country with exchange controls which is authorized to engage in certain specified exchange transactions. In effect, it acts as agent of the central bank in applying exchange control regulations.

Balance of Payments
A statistical tabulation of the financial transactions between the residents of one country and another country, region or a group of countries, the rest of the world, or international institutions.

Bardepot
Literally, 'cash deposit', an ordinance of the German government, in the period 1972–1974, requiring resident companies to put up an interest-free cash deposit against loans or extended payment terms from abroad.

Blocked Account
Currency that is owned by non-residents of an exchange control country and cannot be freely transferred.

Bretton Woods System
The international payments system, based on fixed parities, that was utilized by the members of the International Monetary Fund and which functioned under the rules set forth in the IMF Agreement until 1971.

Broker
A person or firm who arranges the purchase or sale of foreign exchange between banks but is not a principal to the transaction.

Brokerage
Charges made by a broker for services in arranging for the purchase or sale of foreign exchange between banks.

Buying Rate
Rate of exchange at which a bank or dealer will purchase a given foreign currency.

Cable or Telegraphic Transfers (TT)
Payment transactions carried out by use of cable or telegraph, usually internationally, with or without a foreign exchange conversion.

Clearing House Funds
Funds transferred between banks in New York with good value the next business day. International payments in dollars typically are made in the form of clearing house funds.

Closing Rate Method
A method of translating the income statement of a foreign operation whereby all revenue and expenses are translated at the exchange rate prevailing at the end of the period covered by the income statement; also balance sheet consolidation which similarly uses the closing rates of balance sheet data.

Conversion
The exchange of one currency for another.

Covering
The purchase or sale of forward exchange to completely offset the risk of fluctuation in a rate of exchange when payments are to be made or received in that foreign currency in the future.

Courtage
In general, synonymous with brokerage. In Germany, courtage is an exchange fee levied by banks in addition to their commission, even if no broker is used.

Current Rate
In accounting terms, the exchange rate in effect at the balance sheet date of a reporting company.

Depreciation Exchange
A decline in the value of a given currency in terms of one or more other currencies.

Discount
The amount below parity at which spot exchange is sold or the difference between the spot rate and a lower forward rate.

Equilibrium Rate
For spot exchange, the rate that precisely balances the demand and supply of a currency; also, the rate that enables a country to balance its external accounts. For forward exchange, the rate that conforms to the interest parities.

Euro-currencies
Deposits of foreign currencies, denominated in terms of the foreign currency, in domestic banks. Also, lending and borrowing transactions in those currencies. Generally used to denote currencies used for transactions outside their country of origin.

Euro-dollars
Deposits denominated in U.S. dollars in banks outside the United States.

Euro-dollar Markets
A group of markets outside the United States, principally in London, that deals in dollar and other currency deposits maintained outside their country of origin as well as financial transactions in those currencies.

Euro-sterling
Deposits denominated in sterling in banks in non-sterling countries. Also, financial transactions in those deposits.

Exchange Controls or Exchange Restrictions
Limitations to free dealings in foreign exchange or restrictions on the free transfer of domestic currency into foreign currencies and vice versa.

Exchange Gain or Loss
The accounting effect of an exchange rate change.

Exchange Rate
The price of one currency in terms of another at a given moment of time. Also, the middle rates for telegraphic transfers of spot exchange between banks.

Exchange Restrictions
See *Exchange Controls.*

Exchange Risk
The possibility of loss arising from an uncovered (open) position when the related exchange rate rises or falls or the currency is devalued or revalued.

Exposure, Economic
The actual operating effects, short- or long-term, which a company may experience as a currency in which it has commitments, assets or liabilities appreciates or depreciates.

Exposure, Exchange
See *Exchange Risk.*

Federal Funds
Literally, balances of U.S. commercial banks in the Federal Reserve system. Used also to designate funds transferred with immediate good (available) value.

Financial Accounting Standards Board (FASB)
The definitive U.S. accounting body, established in 1974 as the successor to the Accounting Principles Board.

Fixed Exchanges
A system of relatively fixed parities in which exchange rate fluctuations are confined to a specified spread above and below par.

Flexible Exchange Rates or Flexible Exchanges
A system in which wide exchange rate fluctuations are permitted above and below par or in which the parities are frequently adjusted.

Floating Exchange Rates or Floating Exchanges
A system in which either there are no parities, or the parities are not enforced and

the rate of exchange is allowed to fluctuate freely. Rates may still be subject to government intervention to influence their movement.

Fluctuations of Exchange Rates or Exchange Fluctuations
Movement of exchange rates either without limits or within the official support points.

Foreign Balances
Credit balances in accounts abroad held by domestic residents and denominated in foreign currencies. In a broader sense, all liquid foreign short-term assets.

Foreign Bills
Bills of exchange drawn on a foreign resident and denominated in a foreign currency.

Foreign Currency Accounts
Deposit or current accounts denominated in a foreign currency. See also *Hold Accounts* and *Retained Currency Accounts*.

Foreign Currency Translation
The process of expressing amounts denominated or measured in one currency in terms of another currency by use of the exchange rate between the two currencies.

Foreign Exchange
The procedure, methods and institutions involved in exchanging the money of one country into that of another. In a wider sense, all the procedures, documents and institutions involved in transactions between two or more currencies.

Foreign Exchange Brokers
Individuals or firms who act as intermediaries, not principals, between banks for foreign exchange or Euro-dollar transactions and who operate in a local market.

Forward Exchange
The procedures involved in buying or selling foreign exchange for future delivery. Also, foreign currencies bought or sold for future delivery against payment on delivery.

Hedging
Any action taken by a company to eliminate or offset exchange risks that may affect the values of its foreign-currency-denominated assets and liabilities.

Historical Rate
The exchange rate at which foreign currency could be exchanged for the reporting currency at the date a specific transaction or event occurred.

Hold Accounts
Accounts denominated in foreign currency in the name of exporters in an exchange control country and maintained in resident banks.

Hot Money
Funds transferred abroad to avoid inflation or monetary instability at home or to avoid exchange controls, taxation or other regulations.

Inconvertible Currencies
Currencies that are not freely convertible into other currencies for current account transactions by either resident or non-resident holders.

Institute of Chartered Accountants in England and Wales
The definitive U.K. organization for accounting standards, in conjunction with its sister Institutes.

Interbank Sterling
Funds in sterling loaned between London banks, normally in round amounts and without security.

Interest Parity Theory
An economic explanation of the differential between spot and forward rates of exchange. It holds that the differential is a function of the amount that will equalize the interest rates between any two countries.

International Foreign Exchange Market
An informal market that constitutes the focus of a communications network and is located in a principal financial centre of an international trading country and in which foreign exchange is bought and sold and related transactions are carried out. Also, all such markets as a global mechanism.

Intervention, Active
Actual government or official financial agency operation in the foreign exchange markets to prevent, limit or influence changes in rates of exchange.

Intervention Currency
A foreign currency utilized by a government agency to intervene in a foreign exchange market to control or stabilize changes in the exchange value of its currency.

Investment Currencies, Investment Dollar Market
Foreign currency proceeds that are realized from the sale of foreign investments by United Kingdom residents and that can be used for other foreign investments. These in turn form the investment dollar market.

Investment Dollars
Dollars that are realized by U.K. residents from the sale of dollar investments and that are usable for other dollar or foreign currency investments. In a broader sense, all such currencies.

Leads and Lags
Respectively, the acceleration or delay of payments internationally in anticipation of a rise or fall in a rate of exchange.

Long Position
A situation in which assets in a foreign currency exceed liabilities denominated in that currency.

Market, Official
In continental Europe, a designated and officially recognized place where traders meet to execute foreign exchange transactions or to fix daily trading rates of exchange. Also used to designate a regulatory structure in which certain transac-

tions must pass over a controlled, government-supported market and others may be freely negotiated, such as in Belgium.

Non-resident Accounts
Accounts or balances owned by others than the residents of a country or monetary area, thus not directly subject to the latter's exchange control.

Open Position
The difference between long and short positions in a given foreign currency. Also, the difference between the grand totals of all long and short positions.

Optional Forward Contracts
Forward exchange contracts that give one of the parties a choice of delivery dates.

Pars or Parities
The official rate of exchange established by a government with the agreement of the IMF in the case of a member, or unilaterally in the case of a non-member of the IMF.

Premium
The amount paid for spot exchange in excess of par or for forward exchange above the spot rate.

Retained Currency Accounts
Accounts denominated in foreign currency in the name of exporters in exchange control countries, maintained with banks abroad.

Risk, Delivery
The possibility that a seller of foreign exchange may fail to deliver the foreign currency sold after payment has been received in terms of the local currency.

Scheduled Territories
Countries and territories that are members of the sterling area and fall under U.K. Exchange Control regulations. These are at present very few in number.

Settlement Date
The date at which a receivable is or a payment is due. Also, the actual date of delivery of both sides of an exchange transaction.

Short Position
A situation in which liabilities in a foreign currency exceed assets denominated in that currency.

Spot Exchange
The purchase and sale of a foreign currency for immediate delivery (usually for two value days forward) and paid for upon delivery.

Spot Rate
The rate quoted for sale/purchase of one currency against another for immediate delivery (normally two days hence in Western markets).

Spread
(i) The difference between the selling and buying rates for a given currency. (ii) The difference between the support points, or the arbitrage support points, for a

country's currency. (iii) The difference between spot and forward rates for a given currency. (iv) In general, any price differential for a given currency.

Sterling Area
A group of countries that transact their international business in sterling, maintain their international reserves in London, and apply exchange controls similar to those of the United Kingdom. The member countries, which change from time to time, now consist of a few countries that have traditionally employed sterling for international transactions.

Swap
(i) The purchase of spot against the sale of exchange forward exchange. (ii) The sale of spot against the purchase of forward exchange. (iii) The purchase or sale of short against long forward exchange. (iv) The exchange, between government central banks, of deposits to each other's accounts usually to provide foreign exchange to enable each to protect the external value of its currency.

Translation
See *Foreign Currency Translation.*

Undoing Cover or Hedge
The creating of an open, uncovered, or unhedged transaction by the elimination of the transaction that formerly covered or hedged it. Sometimes called unhedging.

Valeur Compensée (Value Compensation) or Here and There
An arrangement whereby payments that arise from foreign exchange transactions are to be made on the same day in the two markets involved. The payer is debited on the date when the payee receives its counterpart, thereby often gaining 2 value days.

Selected Bibliography

The object of this bibliography is to give reference for further reading on any of the main topics of the book. Information on the various elements of exchange exposure can best be sought under the specific problem area, as broken out below:

1. Accounting Aspects
2. Foreign Exchange: (a) theory; (b) markets
3. Rate Forecasting
4. Hedging Strategy
5. Liquidity/Financial Management
6. International Money Management
7. Mathematical Applications
8. Taxation
9. Multinational Companies

1. Accounting Aspects

Accounting conventions applying to the area of exchange risk are set by the professional accounting body, or the legal system of each individual country.

In the U.S.A., the Financial Accounting Standards Board (FASB) is the definitive body, in the U.K. the Accounting Standards Steering Committee (ASSC) of the Institute of Chartered Accountants of England and Wales and its sister Institutes. In certain countries, a statewide regulatory framework — such as the 'Plan Comptable' in France, which has the legal power of legislation — is definitive.

In the U.S.A., the present requirements can be seen in:

Financial Accounting Standards Board, *Statement No. 8 — Accounting for the Translation of Foreign Currency Transactions and Foreign Currency Financial Statements*, October 1975.

An excellent further discussion of the issues is found in the FASB Exposure Draft of December, 1974, with the same title, and in:

Financial Accounting Standards Board, *Accounting for Foreign Currency Translation*. Discussion Memorandum, February 1974.

A description of Canadian practice is given in:

MacDonald Parkinson, *Translation of Foreign Currencies*, The Canadian Institute of Chartered Accountants, 1972.

No precise rules apply in the U.K., as shown in:

Institute of Chartered Accountants, *Recommendations on Accounting Principles*, London, 1975 edition. But see the ASSC Exposure Draft on 'Extraordinary Items and Prior Year Adjustments', September 1975.

Other sources are the large multinational accounting firms, which publish an array of booklets such as:

Price Waterhouse, Information Guide, *Translation Procedures and Foreign Exchange*, December 1974, and professional journals such as *Accountancy* and *Abacus*.

One of the few articles which attempts to show the importance of the various accounting conventions for exchange management is:

Peterson, S. C., 'Impact of accounting methods on foreign exchange management', *Euromoney*, June 1974.

See also:

Flower, J. F., 'Coping with currency fluctuations in company accounts', *Euromoney*, June 1974.

King, Alfred M., 'Budgeting foreign exchange losses', *Management Accounting*, October 1969.

Mandich, Donald R., 'Devaluation, revaluation — re-evaluation?', *Management Accounting*, August 1970.

Two articles dealing with economic exposure as defined in this volume are:

Dufey, Gunter, 'Corporate finance and exchange rate variations', *Financial Management*, June 1972.

Heckerman, Donald, 'The exchange risks of foreign operations', *Journal of Business*, 45, (1), 1972.

2. Foreign Exchange

(a) Theory

The field of foreign exchange is included both in international economic theory and in monetary theory. These coalesce in studies of the international monetary system, although that system itself has changed so rapidly that many good studies are soon outdated. Some of the best classical approaches to exchange/international monetary system theory are found in:

Einzig, Paul, *A Dynamic Theory of Forward Exchange*, London: Macmillan & Co., 1967.

Machlup, Fritz, *International Monetary Economics*, London: George Allen & Unwin Ltd., 1969.

Sohmen, Egon, *Flexible Exchange Rates*, Chicago: University of Chicago, Revised Edition 1969.

Useful studies are:

Aliber, Robert Z., 'Exchange risk, yield curves, and the pattern of capital flows', *The Journal of Finance*, May 1969.

Feldstein, Martin S., 'Uncertainty and forward exchange speculation', *Review of Economics & Statistics*, May 1968.

Inter-Bank Research Organization, *The Rationale and Effectiveness of Exchange Controls on Capital Flows*, London: April 1974.

Ozga, S. A., *The Rate of Exchange and the Terms of Trade*, London: Weidenfeld Goldbacks, 1969.

Schilling, Don, 'Devaluation risk and forward exchange theory', *The American Economic Review*, September 1970.

Schilling, Don, 'Forward exchange and currency position', *Journal of Finance*, December 1969.

Schmitt, Hans O., 'The international monetary system', *International Affairs*, April 1974.

(b) Markets

Here again the problem of dated material arises. The older standard texts are:

Einzig, Paul, *A Textbook of Foreign Exchange*, London: Macmillan & Co., 1970.

Evitt, H. E., *A Manual of Foreign Exchange*, London: Sir Isaac Pitman & Sons Ltd., 1955.

Holmes, Alan R., *The New York Foreign Exchange Market*, New York: Federal Reserve Board 1959.

Walton, L. E., *Foreign Trade and Foreign Exchange*, London: MacDonald & Evans Ltd., 1958.

The best study ever of foreign exchange markets is, in my opinion:

Stein, Jerome L., *The Nature and Efficiency of the Foreign Exchange Market — Essays in International Finance*, No. 40, Princeton: October 1962.

Other useful material, often emanating from practitioners, is found in:

Allen, William R. and Allen, Clark Lee, *Foreign Trade and Finance*, New York: The Macmillan Company, 1959.

Baschnagel, Hubert, 'Fundamentals and technique of foreign exchange dealings', *Finanz und Wirtschaft*, September 1971, January 1972.

Chittenden, George H., *The New York Foreign Exchange Market*, New York: J. P. Morgan & Co., 1957.

Lall, Sanjaya, 'The forward exchange market', *Finance & Development*, September 1967.

Levin, Jay H., 'The Eurodollar market and the international transmission of interest rates', *Canadian Journal of Economics*, Edition 2, May 1974.

Prissert, Pierre, *Le Marché des Changes*, Paris: Sirey, 1972.

Readman, Peter, *et al.*, *The European Money Puzzle*, London: Michael Joseph Ltd., 1973.

Townsend, Charles, 'Are currency exchange costs nibbling at your overseas profits?', *Business Abroad*, February 1970.

Weisweiller, Rudi, *Foreign Exchange*, London: George Allen & Unwin Ltd., 1972.

Whiting, D. P., *Finance of Foreign Trade and Foreign Exchange*, London: MacDonald & Evans Ltd., 1968.

3. Rate Forecasting

This is an area where little applied, as opposed to theoretical, material is available. Summary reviews of the principal problems are found in:

Balassa, Bela, 'The purchasing power parity: a reappraisal' *Journal of Political Economy*, December 1964.

Gailliot, Henry J., 'Purchasing power parity as an explanation of long-term changes in exchange rates' *Journal of Money, Credit and Banking*, August 1970.

Gray, Alan Kirk, 'Foreign exchange forecasting — how far can the computer help?' *Euromoney*, July 1974.

Porter, R. Roderick, 'Forecasting exchange rates' *Euromoney*, September 1973.

Shulman, R. B., 'Are foreign exchange risks measurable?' *Columbia Journal of World Business*, May—June 1970.

Westerfield, Janice M., 'Empirical properties of spot and forward exchange rates' unpublished study, Research Dept., Federal Reserve Bank of Philadelphia, December 1974.

An iconoclastic view is given in:

Dufey, Gunter, and Giddy, Ian H., 'Forecasting exchange rates in a floating world' *Euromoney*, November 1975.

4. Hedging Strategy

As shown in Note 1, Chapter 9, several corporate practitioners have published detailed descriptions of their company's approach to strategy setting.

The field has been given more attention by accountants, businessmen and academicians in recent years. The theoretical work of the latter is listed under

Mathematical Applications, below, while the following articles are representative of the two former sources.

Adams, Robin and Perlman, Robert, 'Long-term contracts in a floating world', *Euromoney*, December 1973.

Bradford, S. R., 'Measuring the cost of forward exchange contracts', *Euromoney*, August 1974.

Furlong, William L., 'Minimizing foreign exchange losses', *Accounting Review*, April 1966.

Korth, Christopher M., 'Survival despite devaluation', *Business Horizons*, April 1971.

May, L. Chester, 'Managing the multinationals' international exchange risks', *The Conference Board RECORD*, October 1975.

Pelli, Guiliano, 'Thoughts on the cost of forward cover in a floating system', *Euromoney*, October 1974.

Prindl, Andreas R., 'Managing exchange exposure in a floating world', *Euromoney*, March 1974.

Prindl, Andreas R., 'Multinational finance', *Accountancy*, December 1974.

Sweeny, H. W. Allen, 'Protective measures against devaluation', *Financial Executive*, January 1968.

Teck, Alan, 'Control your exposure to foreign exchange', *Harvard Business Review*, January—February 1974.

5. Liquidity/financial Management

As mentioned above, an outstanding review of the field of international financial management is found in:

Goeltz, Richard Karl, 'Managing liquid funds on an international scale'. Presentation to the American Management Association Conference on International Cash Management, November 1971.

A number of relevant case studies are found in:

Zenoff, David B. and Zwick, Jack, *International Financial Management*, Englewood Cliffs, New Jersey: Prentice-Hall Inc., 1969.

Another treasurer's look at the field is:

Bardsley, R. Geoffrey, 'Managing international financial transactions', *The International Journal of Accounting*, Fall 1972.

Mathematical applications are voluminous; representative articles are:

Obserteiner, Erich, 'Should the foreign affiliate remit dividends or reinvest?', *Financial Management*, Spring 1973.

Pappas, James L. and Huber, George P., 'Probabilistic short-term financial planning', *Financial Management*, Autumn 1973.

Petty, William J., II and Walker, Ernest W., 'Optimal transfer pricing for the multinational firm', *Financial Management*, Winter 1972.

See also:

Kim, Seung H. and Kuzdrall, Paul J., 'Simulation of financial strategy under fluctuating exchange rates'. Paper presented at the Financial Management Association Meeting, October 16—18, 1975 in Kansas City, Mo.

Meister, Irene W., *Managing the International Financial Function*, New York: National Industrial Conference Board, Inc., 1970.

Robbins, Sidney M. and Stobaugh, Robert B., 'Financing foreign affiliates' *Financial Management*, Winter 1972.

Zenoff, David B., 'Remitting funds from foreign affiliates', *Financial Executive*, March 1968.

6. International Money Management

International Money Management (IMM) combines the fields of cash management, foreign exchange and liquidity management. The rudiments of the field are found in:

Prindl, Andreas R., 'International money management — the environmental framework', *Euromoney*, September, October and November 1971.

Wasserman, Max J., Prindl, Andreas R. and Townsend, Charles C. Jr., *International Money Management*, New York: American Management Association, 1972.

Other sources are:

Brooke, Michael and Mitton, Alan, 'How to manage multinationals', *Management Today*, July 1974.

Neubert, Helmut, *Totales Cash-Flow-System und Finanzflussverfahren*, Wiesbaden: Gabler, 1974.

Plasschaert, Sylvain, 'Emerging patterns of financial management in multinational companies', *Economisch en Sociaal Tijdschrift*, December 1971.

Prindl, Andreas R., 'Financial management in the multinationals', *Euromoney*, April 1975.

Smith, Dan Throop, 'Financial variables in international business', *Harvard Business Review*, January 1966.

Wooster, John T. and Thoman, G. Richard, 'New financial priorities for MNCs', *Harvard Business Review*, May—June 1974.

7. Mathematical Applications

Folks, William R. Jr., 'Decision analysis for exchange risk management', *Financial Management* Winter 1972.

Levy, Ferdinand K., 'An application of heuristic problem solving to accounts receivable management', *Management Science*, February 1966.

Lietaer, Bernard A., 'Managing risks in foreign exchange', *Harvard Business Review*, March—April 1970.

Lietaer, Bernard A., *Financial Management of Foreign Exchange*, Cambridge (Mass), MIT Press 1971.

Ness, Walter L. Jr., 'A linear programming approach to financing the multinational corporation', *Financial Management*, Winter 1972.

Rutenberg, David P., 'Maneuvering liquid assets in a multinational company: Formulation and deterministic solution procedures', *Management Science*, June 1970.

Shapiro, Alan, 'Exchange rate changes, inflation and the value of the multinational corporation', *Journal of Finance* May 1975.

Srinivasan, V., 'A transshipment model for cash management decisions', *Management Science*, June 1974.

Thore, Sten, 'Credit networks', *Economica*, February 1969.

8. Taxation

Here again the local tax laws, authorities and counsel of each country should be consulted. For U.S. purposes, a recent comprehensive study is:

Ravenscroft, Donald R., *Taxation and Foreign Currency*, Cambridge, Massachusetts: The Law School of Harvard University, 1973.

A general guide to the field with a British orientation is:

Chown, John F., *Taxation and Multinational Enterprise*, London: Longman Group Limited, 1974.

Many accounting firms publish a tax guide to each major country for their clients. Among them are Price Waterhouse, Arthur Andersen and Ernst and Ernst.

Professional journals such as *Tax Executive* have pertinent articles from time to time, particularly as tax law concerning exposure is as volatile as the exchange markets. Specific articles of that genre are:

Burge, Marianne, 'Devaluation and its tax consequences', *Quarterly Review*, July 1969.

Curtiss, Daniel W., 'Hedging balance-sheet exposure after tax', *Euromoney*, April 1975.

Ernst and Ernst, 'Financial aspects of foreign currency devaluation and revaluation', *International Business Series Special Report Number 3*, December 1969.

Financial Times Tax Newsletter, 'Taxation and exchange rate fluctuations', September 1972.

Nicholson, Gordon J., 'Tax problems resulting from devaluation', *Tax Executive*, October 1968.

Stam, Colin F., *Essays on Taxation*, New York: Tax Foundation Inc., 1974.

See also:

Frommel, S. N., *Taxation of Branches and Subsidiaries in Western Europe, Canada and the U.S.A.*, London: Kluwer-Harrap, 1975.

9. Multinational Companies

Foreign Policy Research Institute, *Multinational Corporation — Nation-State Interaction*, Washington, 1971.

is itself an annotated and precise bibliography on the multinational company through 1971. A descriptive bibliography is also given in:

Ewing, David W., 'MNCs on trial', *Harvard Business Review*, May—June 1972.

A widely read descriptive study, under the framework of a long-term Harvard Business School research project, is:

Robbins, Sidney M. and Stobaugh, Robert B., *Money in the Multinational Enterprise*, London: Longman, 1974.

The role of multinationals in international trade and finance and their effect on local economics is, of course, widely debated. Two general and apposite conclusions are found in:

United Nations, *The Impact of Multinational Corporations on Development and on International Relations*, New York, 1974.

U.S. Tariff Commission, *Implications of Multinational Firms for World Trade and Investment and for U.S. Trade and Labor*, Washington, February 1973.

The *Economist's* study of 1972 is thought-provoking:

Macrae, Norman, 'Multinational business — the future of international business', *The Economist*, Sept. 1972.

See also:

Gabriel, Peter P. 'MNCs in the third world: Is conflict unavoidable?', *Harvard Business Review*, July—August 1972.

Levinson, Charles, *Capital, Inflation and the Multinationals*, London: George Allen & Unwin Ltd., 1971.

Manser, W. A. P., *The Financial Role of Multi-National Enterprises*, London: Associated Business Programmes, 1973.

Rolfe, Sidney E. and Damm, Walter (Eds), *The Multinational Corporation in the World Economy*, New York: Praeger, 1970.

Tugendhat, Christopher, *The Multinationals*, London: Eyre & Spottiswoode, 1971.

U.S. Senate, Subcommittee on Multinational Corporations, *Multinational Corporations in the Dollar Devaluation Crisis*, Washington: June, 1975.

Index